REVOLUTION
in the Church

Russell Burrill

HART RESEARCH CENTER
FALLBROOK, CALIFORNIA

Edited by Ken McFarland
Cover art direction and design by Ed Guthero
Cover illustration by Bryant Eastman

The author assumes full responsibility for the accuracy of
all facts, quotations, and references as cited in this book.

ISBN 1-878046-29-2

Contents

Foreword

There seem to be two kinds of people in the pews these days—those who are bored, and those who are praying for change. Few are satisfied. George Barna's recent study of Protestant clergy indicates that most are not enthusiastic about what is happening in their congregations, and my own research with Adventist pastors indicates that many feel the same way. It is time for this book!

What can the church be? What are our hopes and dreams for the Adventist Church in North America and around the world? What is God's will for His remnant church today? With the care of a Bible scholar, the heart of a pastor, and the passion of an evangelist, Russell Burrill lays out a clear answer to these questions.

It is one thing to pray for revival and reformation. It is another thing to envision how the church will be changed by revival and reformation. Russell Burrill has done the latter. He is a visionary leader with a strong sense of the kind of church God wants Adventist congregations to be at the end of the twentieth century.

Ministry is a verb. Ministry describes what church members do, not a segment of the church structure. The "consumer church" attitude of today has turned the clergy into performers—providers of a certain kind of service—and the *laos*, or people of God, into customers who sit back to be served. This is not biblical. It is sub-Christian. It is the scandal of our time.

This volume contains a painstaking record from scripture and Adventist history to document this indictment. It will be an eye-opening set of facts for many people. But the book does more than that. It also asks the question, If this is true, how does that change what happens in your local church from week to week? It gives a detailed prescription for the outpouring of the Holy Spirit in a local church.

Many who speak and write about the Holy Spirit and His role in the church focus entirely on an elusive quality of spirituality. Sometimes they are accused of seeking an unrealistic "high." These are often personalities who have little interest in the practicality of church life and the hard work of ministering to hurting people.

Revolution in the Church focuses on the real work of the Holy Spirit in the life of the believer and the congregation—bestowing gifts for ministry. More information is shared here than has previously been published anywhere on the crucial subjects pastors and lay leaders are asking for—how to keep the gifts of the Spirit alive, how to bring about a new start in your church, how to develop an empowering program of training and support for lay ministry.

This book will be encouraging for agents of change, and it will be painful for those who see the church as essentially a bastion for ritual and tradition. Russell Burrill uses the word "revolution" in the title of this book because the principles he reveals from Scripture and the writings of Ellen White will, if taken seriously, completely turn around the ideas about church that have been taken for granted for decades.

Change is not easy. Human nature resists it, even when it is God's will. No time of real revival and reformation has come upon the church at any point in history without conflict. But this should not be a reason to ignore the call of the Holy Spirit.

Don't jump to conclusions. Much of the current conflict

that gets a lot of notice among Adventists has nothing to do with the issues raised here. In many of the current controversies, it would not matter to the mission of the church if one side or the other prevailed completely. In fact, many of the agitators and debaters who churn out journals, documents, and newsletters—and who are always looking for speaking appointments—are simply out of touch with what God is really attempting to do among His remnant people today. They are too concerned with obscure ideas or are really involved in a game of "holier-than-thou" and thus cannot hear the still, small voice revealed in these pages.

It is also true that this book is not about quick, simple solutions. No panacea boxed with an easy-to-read recipe will be found here. This is a call to the life of discipleship, not only as individual believers, but as congregations. It is "a long obedience in the same direction." It is always focused, as is Jesus, not on the feelings of the saints, but on the needs of the unsaved.

Neither conservatives nor liberals may like this book. It challenges the complacency of the liberals and the tradition of the conservatives. It will find a response from those who want fully to follow Christ and to see His power poured out in the Adventist Church as we approach the second advent. It will be a deep spring in a dry desert for many, many local church leaders.

I have high hopes for what will happen when you read this book. It is my prayer that the Holy Spirit will use it to bring a new vision to pastors, elders, and church board members—and new life to congregations.

Monte Sahlin
Associate Director of Church Ministries
Seventh-day Adventist Church in North America
June 1993

About the Author

Russell Burrill is the Director of the North American Division Evangelism Institute in Berrien Springs, Michigan. He has served not only as a pastor and evangelist in many parts of the United States, but is also in great demand as a speaker and trainer.

In addition to presenting seminars on Bible prophecy to thousands across the United States and Canada and in overseas countries, Russell is at the forefront of today's renewed emphasis in the church on small-group fellowships, spiritual gift-based church ministry, and lay evangelism.

This volume is the result of many requests he has received to put into book form his insights on lay ministry, spiritual gifts, and small-group dynamics.

Acknowledgments

I wish to acknowledge the many people with whom I have interacted over the years who have shaped my opinions. The many books I have read on this subject and the numerous seminars I have attended have also greatly influenced the ideas expressed in this book.

I wish it were possible to give credit to each one who has influenced me, but it is impossible for me to trace the origin of many of the ideas I've shared here. If I have used any material without giving proper credit, that has been unintentional. After I have thoroughly digested a concept, I come to feel it is my own. Yet I recognize that I may be indebted to someone else for those conclusions. Many of the ideas expressed here have germinated from my reading of the the writings of Ellen White. While I did not quote her extensively in this book, I acknowledge my indebtedness to her for much of what appears here.

Furthermore, I wish to especially thank my secretary, Mrs. Genevieve Clark, and my wife, Cynthia Burrill, for helping prepare the manuscript for publication. Their many hours of labor are deeply appreciated.

Finally, I pray that the ideas expressed in this book will have a profound impact on the many local Seventh-day Adventist churches in North America. It is my prayer that God will use this book to bring the church back to its roots and revolutionize it for the twenty-first century.

—The author

1

Igniting the Fire

Revival fires! How the church longs for the Holy Spirit to enliven it for the final accomplishment of its mission!

Adventism was born as a dynamic, mission-centered movement. Passion for sharing the message reigned in the minds and hearts of the early pioneers. They labored until bone weary; they sacrificed health and possessions in attempting to reach the world with the saving news of Jesus Christ and the third angel's message. Mission drove them! Mission motivated them! Mission was the flame that burned within them!

Nearly 150 years later, the Adventist church prepares to enter the third millennium of the Christian era. What has happened to mission? Where are the revival fires of the first-century church and early Adventism? Are they still burning? If one examines world-wide Adventism today, the answer is an unmistakable "yes." Adventism is alive and well and growing at an astounding pace in the third world. Yet in North America, Western Europe, and Australia, we find a different story. As Adventism burns with intense heat in the third world, it barely flames in its homelands.

At times, North America appears to retreat rather than advance. Financial difficulties have led to cutbacks in ministerial personnel, dissident groups on the fringes of Adventism have wrought havoc in many local churches, and indifference has dulled the minds of many members. "Cultural Adventism" allows these to enjoy the Adventist lifestyle and associate with their Adventist friends but to have little or no apparent concern for mission.

Yet, beneath this pessimism, there burns still in the Adventist psyche a tremendous desire to see the work of God finished. The dynamic explosion of evangelism in the former Soviet Union has captivated the Adventist mind. Perhaps even in North America similar results might be seen.

Desire is one thing; action is another. Some feel that all we can do is to pray for the outpouring of the Holy Spirit. Yet few even realize what that entails. Others seem satisfied with small accomplishments, hoping that someday the real breakthrough will occur.

It is the thesis of this book that both are necessary. We must not only pray and receive the outpouring of the Holy Spirit, we must also prepare for the Holy Spirit to use us in finishing the work of God. This may mean a drastic change in how we are accustomed to "doing church." It *will* mean that we will have to stop "playing church" and get down to the business of being the church of God.

The tragedy of the church in North America is that it has copied much of its way of doing things from surrounding popular Protestant churches. But God intends that the Adventist church function in a totally different way. Hiring pastors to do the work of the ministry while the laity pay, attend, and observe is not God's plan for the Adventist church. In fact, this practice has resulted in the present Laodicean condition.

We need to witness a rebirth of the laity concurrent with a wholehearted preparation for the outpouring of the Holy

Spirit. Laity must once again become "the church." Likewise, pastors need to revise their church role and return to their biblical job description—as a trainer of the laity. Until this happens, we can pray endlessly for the latter rain, and it will not fall. There must be action as well as prayer to restore the church to its biblical base, with laity and clergy working together as a team.

> The work of God in the earth can never be finished until the men and women comprising our church membership rally to the work and unite their efforts with those of ministers and church officers.—*Gospel Workers,* pp. 351, 352.

Let's explore both the need for receiving the Holy Spirit and the involvement of the laity in the work of the ministry. There have been many excellent books and articles written on the need for the Holy Spirit; therefore the focus of this book will be on the part we have somewhat neglected: involvement of the laity. Yet we cannot ignore the connection between the two. Before we examine a new understanding of the involvement of laity in the church, we first need to discover our great need of the Holy Spirit.

The Holy Spirit in Action

Some may believe that the reception of the Holy Spirit will take place in a large meeting of the church. These perhaps imagine a warm, glowing feeling possessing us, tears being shed and sins confessed, and the church leaving such a meeting with renewed power.

Without denying that the Holy Spirit could be poured out in such a manner, we must understand the purpose for the outpouring of the Holy Spirit. The Holy Spirit is not given to create warm feelings but to renew us with power for witnessing. That is why it is hard to imagine the outpouring of the Holy Spirit without an enlightened and involved laity.

The Holy Spirit supernaturally enables the church to accomplish its mission to reach the world for Christ. We can never divorce the Holy Spirit from the mission of the church. This was the whole reason for the outpouring of the Holy Spirit.

Jesus, before returning to the Father, summed up His chief concerns in "the great commission":

> Then Jesus came to them and said, "All authority in heaven and on earth has been given to me. Therefore go and make disciples of all nations, baptizing them in the name of the Father and of the Son and of the Holy Spirit, and teaching them to obey everything I have commanded you. And surely I am with you always, to the very end of the age." —Matthew 28:18-20, NIV.

Note that the concern of Jesus was not just the fulfillment of mission, but also the reception of the Holy Spirit's power to enable the church to accomplish that mission. The church was not simply to go into all the world with the message of Christ; they were to go in the power of the Holy Spirit.

Each Gospel writer connects the accomplishment of Christ's mission with receiving the power of the Holy Spirit. Note Jesus' last words:

> He said to them, "Go into all the world and preach the good news to all creation. Whoever believes and is baptized will be saved, but whoever does not believe will be condemned. And these signs will accompany those who believe: In my name they will drive out demons; they will speak in new tongues; they will pick up snakes with their hands; and when they drink deadly poison, it will not hurt them at all; they will place their hands on sick people, and they will get well." —Mark 16:15-18, NIV.

"And repentance and forgiveness of sins will be preached in his name to all nations, beginning at Jerusalem. You are witnesses of these things. I am going to send you what my Father has promised; but stay in the city until you have been clothed with power from on high."—Luke 24:47-49, NIV.

On one occasion, while he was eating with them, he gave them this command: "Do not leave Jerusalem, but wait for the gift my Father promised, which you have heard me speak about. For John baptized with water, but in a few days you will be baptized with the Holy Spirit." So when they met together, they asked him, "Lord, are you at this time going to restore the kingdom to Israel?" He said to them, "It is not for you to know the times or the dates the Father has set by his own authority. But you will receive power when the Holy Spirit comes on you; and you will be my witnesses in Jerusalem, and in all Judea and Samaria, and to the ends of the earth."—Acts 1:4-8, NIV.

As Jesus ended His ministry and returned to the Father, the overwhelming obsession that stirred His soul was the need for the disciples to fulfill His mission and their need for power to do it.

Judaism of the first century had become an exclusive club of people who thought they possessed the truth. Salvation, they believed, was assured as long as they had membership in the seed of Abraham. Jesus came and disturbed their exclusiveness, calling them to account for their failure to fulfill His mission.

Now Jesus was concerned lest the same thing happen to the Christian church. It was not our Lord's purpose that the church become a navel-gazing institution. He had called this new body into existence for one purpose: to make disciples among all ethnic groups. His was a clarion call for commitment to that mission. And for its accomplishment, He promised them the enabling power of the Holy Spirit.

In this initial endowment of the Holy Spirit, we discover its purpose: empowerment for the accomplishment of mission. The Holy Spirit is poured out for action—for the accomplishment of the task of Christ. We must never see the outpouring of the Holy Spirit as separate from its great function—the making of disciples. That's why we cannot finish the work without the Holy Spirit. The Spirit cannot be poured out unless there are people willing to be filled with power, enabling them to share Christ with the world around them.

The early disciples spent ten days praying for the deluge of the Holy Spirit. The instruments were ready to be used by God. The Holy Spirit was poured out upon the waiting company, and immediately they became involved in the fulfillment of Christ's mission. Again, there is no separating the Holy Spirit from the accomplishment of mission.

How was the Holy Spirit manifested in the early church? In response to what Christ Himself had promised in Mark 16:15-18, miraculous signs and wonders occurred with increasing rapidity. The disciples spoke in new languages (Acts 2:1-4), the sick were healed, and miracles occurred. All of these were spiritual gifts that empowered the church for action.

The New Testament seems to emphasize the more miraculous of those spiritual gifts: tongues, healings, and miracles, for example. Yet the New Testament indicates that non-miraculous spiritual gifts were also imparted by the Holy Spirit (Romans 12:6-8).

Since we now live in the dispensation of the Holy Spirit, we can expect the same spiritual gifts that were so active in the New Testament church to be active in the remnant church. Yet strangely, Adventists have sometimes avoided spiritual gifts and have been almost afraid of the more miraculous spiritual gifts. Perhaps this arises from our concern not to be deceived by the counterfeit. However, we must not be so frightened of the counterfeit that we reject the genuine outpouring of the Holy Spirit in our midst. Such a rejection would be even more amazing because of the heavy emphasis early Adventists placed on spiritual gifts—especially the miraculous gift of prophecy manifested in the writings of Ellen White.

For a church that was so blessed with one spiritual gift (prophecy) in its early days, it is strange indeed to be overly concerned today about the manifestation of spiritual gifts in our midst. We pray much for the outpouring of the Holy Spirit in the latter rain. But what is the latter rain but an intensification of the early rain of Pentecost? In this first explosion of the Holy Spirit's power, the Holy Spirit manifested Himself by pouring out spiritual gifts upon His church, including the more miraculous gifts. Should we not expect that the latter rain will witness the same thing?

In the latter part of this book, we will explore in depth the subject of spiritual gifts as a demonstration of the Holy Spirit's power. If we are to be ready for this final outpouring of the Spirit upon the church, we need to restructure our churches for the reception of spiritual gifts. Then, as the Holy Spirit is poured out upon God's last-day church, our congregations will be ready to receive all the gifts that God sends.

In addition to dispensing spiritual gifts, the Holy Spirit empowers God's church through the fruit of the Spirit:

> But the fruit of the Spirit is love, joy, peace,
> patience, kindness, goodness, faithfulness,
> gentleness and self-control. Against such things
> there is no law.—Galatians 5:22, 23, NIV.

The fruit of the Spirit, as well as the gifts of the Spirit, enable the church to accomplish its mission in pentecostal power. The difference between the charismatic emphasis on spiritual gifts and the function of spiritual gifts as set forth in the Bible is that charismatics tend to see the gifts as primarily for producing feelings of spiritual ecstasy, whereas the Bible describes these gifts as given for the accomplishment of mission. Remember, Pentecost resulted in tremendous church growth; so will the last-day Pentecost. Any manifestation of the gifts of the Spirit that does not result in souls won to Jesus is a counterfeit.

While the supernatural gifts of the Spirit call the attention of the world to God's remnant people, the fruit of the Spirit demonstrates through them the perfect character of Christ. God cannot call the attention of the world to the remnant as long as they are fighting one another. This can only happen if they reflect the character of Christ. Ellen White graphically stated it this way:

> Christ is waiting with longing desire for the manifestation of Himself in His church. When the character of Christ shall be perfectly reproduced in His people, then He will come to claim them as His own.—*Christ's Object Lessons*, p. 69.

The Bible declares God's character to be love (1 John 4:8). Love is the first fruit of the Spirit. The result of God's people reflecting the character of Christ—a loving and lovable people of God—is the fulfillment of the mission of Christ. Notice as Ellen White continues:

> Were all who profess His name bearing fruit to His glory, how quickly the whole world would be sown with the seed of the gospel. Quickly, the last great harvest would be ripened and Christ would come to gather the precious grain.—*Ibid*.

> If we would humble ourselves before God, and be kind and courteous and tenderhearted and pitiful, there would be one hundred conversions to the truth where now there is only one.—*Testimonies for the Church*, vol. 9, p. 189.

The greatest need facing the Seventh-day Adventist Church today is to receive the Holy Spirit. To receive that power will do two things for the church: it will produce the fruit of the Spirit, and it will empower the church through the gifts of the Spirit.

Yet we must not wait until some future time when the Holy Spirit will be poured out in this latter-rain power. If we are not now receiving the Holy Spirit so that our lives produce both the fruit and the gifts, we will not receive the latter rain when it shall fall.

Could it be that somehow in the "way" we conduct "church" today we are making it difficult for the Holy Spirit to perform both of these works in His remnant body? It is this author's contention that it is time for a total restructuring of how we "do church" on the local level. In the pages that follow we will examine a new structure of the church based on the laity and clergy performing their biblical roles.

It is also the author's contention that this return to a biblical model of the church will help unleash the baptism of the Spirit and help free the church to become the channel for the final display of the character of God to the world.

As Ellen White noted in a quotation cited at the beginning of this chapter, this work cannot be finished until laity and clergy unite. It's high time for that to begin.

2

Calling All Laity

Imagine a church on fire with the power of the Holy Spirit. What would such a church look like? Would it look like *your* Seventh-day Adventist church? How would it be different?

In my mind's eye, I can picture such a church—a church fully partaking of pentecostal power. The Holy Spirit is being poured out superabundantly, and people are flocking to the church from all directions. The members are alive with the gospel of Christ. Their services are not dead formalism, but are alive with the Holy Spirit's power as members share week by week what Jesus has been doing in their lives. Each Sabbath the church is rejoicing over new people who have come to know Christ through the ministry of the laity. In this imaginary church, every member has a ministry. There are no idlers, for to be a Christian in this church means to be involved in meaningful ministry for the Master. Love, joy, and peace are seen in the members of this church as they reflect the character of Christ to their community. And the community responds to the demonstration of real love. As a result, the church is known as the one place in the community where one can find love and acceptance.

Don't you wish your church were like this? Who wouldn't want to be a part of such a church! The world would break the doors down trying to get in. If you had lived in the first century, this would have been a normal church. Yet here at the end of the twentieth century we would view such a church as abnormal and unusual. This need not be, for it is God's desire that His church at the end of the age be as dynamic and alive, as loving and caring, and as involved in ministry, as was the first-century church. What, then, is God's role for the laity in His church?

The Priesthood of All Believers

God's ideal for His people is found in the garden of Eden. Here, unencumbered by sin, God's initial creation held face-to-face communion with their Maker. Nothing separated Adam and Eve from intimate communion with God. In the cool of the evening, Adam and Eve entered into direct discussion with the infinite God of the universe. That's our God—the God of relationships.

Then that relationship was broken. Adam and Eve distrusted their Maker and sinned. One of the consequences was the loss of that intimate communion with God they had enjoyed. No longer did they enjoy their original Edenic relationship with God; no longer could their descendants approach God directly. Instead, a system of intermediaries was introduced. Chosen ones interceded on behalf of the people, since they no longer had face-to-face communion with God. Initially the first-born became the intermediary; later, the patriarchs; and finally, at the Exodus event, the priests.

Old Testament priests performed two tasks that the people were unable to perform for themselves: First, they served as intermediaries—as go-betweens. When ancient Israel sinned, they did not directly approach God for forgiveness. Instead, they brought a lamb to the priest, who took their sacrifice into the sanctuary. Second, the priests performed ministry for the people. The common people were not allowed to enter the sanctuary, but the priests were admitted. The high priest alone could venture into the Most Holy Place, and he could do that only once each year.

Thus, the functions of intercession and ministry were reserved exclusively for the priests in Old Testament times. Yet this was not God's ideal. It was only a stop-gap measure provided for a time until Christ could come and restore what Adam had lost. Remember, in Eden each person had the privilege of direct communion with God and direct ministry for God. No one needed the services of a mediatorial priest; they were "priests" themselves.

When Adam sinned, this privilege was lost to the human race. In God's plan, the redemptive ministry of Christ was to restore the Edenic relationship to those redeemed by the blood of Jesus. Calvary ended the Old Testament priestly system and restored the doctrine of the priesthood of all believers.

This is the joy of new life in Christ. Because of His redemptive ministry, the believer has direct access to God and all the rights of the ministry. No longer is direct access and ministry to be the exclusive domain of the clergy. The privilege of living in the New Testament era is that every Christian can be his own priest. Note how John the Revelator glories in this new status for the believer:

> And from Jesus Christ, who is the faithful witness, the firstborn from the dead, and the ruler of the kings of the earth. To him who loves us and has freed us from our sins by his blood, and has made us to be a kingdom and priests to serve his God and Father—to him be glory and power for ever and ever! Amen.—Revelation 1:5, 6, NIV.

> And they sang a new song: "You are worthy to take the scroll and to open its seals, because you were slain, and with your blood you purchased

men for God from every tribe and language and
people and nation. You have made them to be a
kingdom and priests to serve our God, and they
will reign on the earth."—Revelation 5:9, 10, NIV.

Note particularly the connection between the redemptive ministry of Christ on the cross and the restoration of
the doctrine of the priesthood of all believers. The New
Testament announces in unmistakable terms the restoration of that which Adam lost—the privilege of every believer
to be a priest before God. The death of Christ on Golgotha's
hill has ended forever the priestly class. Christ has broken
down every wall, including the wall that separated the clergy
from the laity. In Christ's kingdom there is only one class—
the priestly class into which all believers are born when they
accept Jesus Christ as their Redeemer.

The apostle Peter, writing to Gentile Christians scattered
throughout the Roman empire, declares all believers to be
the royal priesthood:

You also, like living stones, are being built into
a spiritual house to be a holy priesthood, offering
spiritual sacrifices acceptable to God through
Jesus Christ.—1 Peter 2:5, NIV.

But you are a chosen people, a royal priesthood,
a holy nation, a people belonging to God, that you
may declare the praises of him who called you out of
darkness into his wonderful light.—1 Peter 2:9, NIV.

According to Peter, all Christians belong to the priesthood. In the New Testament, the church does not *have* a
priesthood—it *is* a priesthood. The priesthood of all believers is the only authorized priesthood in the New Testament.
Here we have the full restoration of that which Adam lost.
All God's children now have direct access to God, and all
God's children have a right to ministry. That right has been
fully established by Christ's redemptive ministry.

Since every believer is a priest, Peter declares that each believer must now offer a spiritual sacrifice to God. This sacrifice he claims is their rightful service as believers. What is this sacrifice that the believer must offer? The apostle Paul answers that question clearly in Romans 12:1 (NIV):

> Therefore, I urge you, brothers, in view of God's mercy, to offer your bodies as living sacrifices, holy and pleasing to God—this is your spiritual act of worship.

The sacrifice that Christians are called to offer is not bulls, goats, and sheep, but their bodies, which they give in loving ministry for the Master. Paul maintains that this is their reasonable service.

According to Paul and Peter, ministry is not only the right and privilege of every New Testament believer, it is a natural result of being a Christian. The New Testament church could not even imagine a Christian who was not involved in ministry. It was inherent in the theology of the first Christians. It was their right and privilege because of Christ's death for them.

Somehow in this modern age, we have largely divorced ministry from basic Christianity. The idea has gained acceptance that it is possible to be a Christian and not be involved in ministry. Ministry, some have even dared to claim, is the responsibility of the clergy, and even some clergy have cautioned laypeople to avoid entering their domain. Performing ministry, however, is not the prerogative of the clergy alone; it is, instead, the rightful domain of all believers. That right was the legacy of Christ's death on Golgotha's hill. Limiting ministry to clergy is totally foreign to the New Testament church.

It was impossible for New Testament believers not to be involved in meaningful ministry in harmony with their spiritual gifts. In fact, the whole context of Romans 12 is a discussion of spiritual gifts. The involvement of every member in ministry in harmony with their spiritual gifts was the norm for the first-century church, and this likewise must become the norm of God's last-day church.

Implications of "Every Member a Priest"

Adventists have always believed in the doctrine of the priesthood of all believers. Like all Protestants, we have accepted this teaching as part of our Reformation heritage. Yet even the Reformers failed to see the full significance of accepting this doctrine. Some saw it in theory but failed to put it into practice.

The most basic implication of accepting this doctrine is the understanding that every believer has direct access to the Father through Jesus Christ. There is only one Mediator between us and God—Jesus (1 Timothy 2:5). No Adventist would think of going to his or her pastor and asking for forgiveness of sin. Any pastor who attempted to grant such forgiveness would no doubt lose his credentials. It is anathema for us even to think of going through any mediator except Christ to receive forgiveness of sins because of our strong belief in the doctrine of the priesthood of all believers.

Yet the mediatorial service between God and the people was only one of the duties of the Old Testament priest. As we have seen, the Hebrew priest also performed ministry for the people because they were unable to perform it for themselves. This is the part of the doctrine the Reformers saw but failed to fully implement in the church. Yet early Adventism actually implemented part of the doctrine. Tragically, modern Adventists have failed to recognize its significance. And it is this second aspect of the doctrine of the priesthood of all believers that we desperately need to restore if we are serious about finishing the work of God.

If every member is a priest, then every Christian really is a minister and therefore has a ministry to perform. Once people accept the New Testament teaching of the priesthood of all believers, they must accept the fact that as priests, all believers have a ministry, and all must discover their ministry or be regarded as unfaithful Christians. This understanding of the doctrine of the priesthood of all believers helps eliminate artificial distinctions that have arisen between laity and clergy. Since every Christian is a minister, clergy do not have a higher standing with God than laity. Clergy prayers rise no higher than laity prayers.

Sadly, many laypeople have viewed their pastors as being on a higher spiritual level than they, simply because of their function as clergy. If we correctly understand the priesthood of all believers, we will realize that there is no difference in status between clergy and laity. We are all on the same level. However, there is a functional difference between laity and clergy. In another chapter we will consider this difference as we examine the biblical job description of the pastor. However, at this point, let it be clearly stated that the function of the laity, biblically, is the performance of ministry. Whenever people are performing ministry, they are acting in the capacity of laity—even if they belong to the clergy!

The New Testament church functioned with the equality of clergy and laity, since it recognized every believer as a priest. Thus, this doctrine—with all its ramifications—means that we as a church must once again recognize that the Christian life is a ministry. And this ministry is the sole right of all believers.

How Clergy Usually Motivate Laity

Since many within the church have been operating on an incorrect theology—that clergy are hired to do the work of the ministry—the accomplishment of the church's mission has been hindered. Clergy have at times felt that they must involve laity in ministry, but they have not been willing to fully release people for ministry or to allow them to perform significant service. This has occurred because the clergy have viewed ministry as an *activity* rather than as a *way of life* for the believer.

As a result, the clergy dream up programs to involve the laity. These programs may not even be in harmony with the spiritual gifts of the members. Since the members have not been involved in the planning of such programs, they have no great desire to be a part of them. But the clergy need their help. So the pastor may preach a sermon on witnessing that makes everyone feel guilty. With this heavy guilt trip weighing on them, laity show up for the pastor's program—until the guilt wears off. Then the pastor has to preach another sermon, producing even more guilt. Again the faithful few show up. Eventually, the guilt rolls off the heads of the rest of the congregation, and it affects very few.

This method produces discouraged pastors who feel that the laity are lazy and don't want to be involved. The laity, on the other hand, wander about with increasingly heavy guilt, feeling that they ought to be involved, but growing increasingly uncomfortable with guilt-based ministry.

We wonder why the work is stymied when this is being repeated in church after church. Was this typical of the witnessing of the early church? Did they carry out their witnessing programs by brow-beating people? Absolutely not! To them, witnessing was a way of life, because every believer had a ministry, and the entire church worked together and realized that each person had his place in God's church. There was a special work for all. Some were front-line soldiers, out there confronting the world for Christ. Others were back-up troops, helping care for new converts, integrating them into the fellowship of the church—and keeping other members supplied. Others were generals and administrators who kept the whole church running. Each had a place and a special ministry.

In the early church, it was recognized that every member had a spiritual gift or a combination of gifts. All did not possess the same gifts. God had enough gifts in the church to make it function properly. He placed each believer in a particular church because that person had a gift which the congregation needed at that time. Every believer was important and needed.

When each Christian discovers his or her gift and engages in ministry, there is no frustration because of mismatched gifts and service. Everyone is happy with a gift-based ministry. The church grows naturally as a result. That's why it is so important for each believer to discover his or her spiritual gifts. When this happens, members will not look down on someone who has a different gift from theirs. They will work as a team to get the job done.

> To everyone work has been allotted and no one
> can be a substitute for another. — *Christian
> Service*, p. 10.

It is this concept of clergy/lay-team ministry that needs to be recaptured in today's Adventism. As we pattern our ministry after the New Testament model, we will need to help members find their ministry in harmony with their spiritual gifts. Only a gift-based ministry can adequately fulfill the New Testament model of lay ministry.

Most of us think that the climax of all we do as a church is focused on Sabbath morning.

> But the doctrine of the priesthood of all believers
> indicates that for the Christian the *climax* is what is
> done *in the world during the week!* What happens
> on Sabbath is to prepare him for this ministry in the
> world during the week. — Dr. Rex D. Edwards,
> *Every Believer a Minister*, p. 114.[1]

We must move beyond the concept that the only place ministry occurs is in the church. The biblical concept of ministry sees the believer's entire life as ministry. The function of the church is to better prepare the believer for his or her ministry. It is in that sense that the church must be seen as a training center for Christian ministry.

Difference Between Clergy and Laity

The early church began as a lay movement. Not one of the early disciples was a trained clergy person. All of the early leaders were lay people. The twelve were set apart to devote full time to the work of the ministry, but they were still lay people and not a notch above the other disciples. The New Testament does ordain a full-time ministry, but not with the status distinctions so apparent today between laity and clergy.

In the New Testament, the clergy were lay people who devoted full time to directing gospel work. The laity were seen as the performers of ministry and the clergy as the trainers and equippers of ministry. Yet, as part of the laity, the clergy also performed ministry.

As the church advanced into the Dark Ages, the clergy were gradually elevated to a higher standing in the minds of the people, until eventually the priesthood developed, and the role of the laity became limited to paying the bills and observing the clergy perform their ministry.

Medieval Christianity totally obscured the role of the laity. The result was that laity were manipulated and used but were never a vital part of the church.

This status differentiation was even carried over into Protestantism. As a result, the laity's role in much of the modern church has been reduced to serving as spectators, whose main religious function is to occupy a pew on Sabbath morning. As long as members show up on Sabbath morning, they are considered to be in good and regular standing. In the New Testament church, that was anathema. They could never have even envisioned a Christian who was not actively engaged in ministry.

In most churches today, the clergy perform most of the ministry while the laity watch. Fortunately, in some churches, ministry involvement has been expanded to include a few key laypeople, but few churches have expanded ministry to include all the laity. Consequently, in most churches frustration develops at nominating committee time, because seemingly no one wants to become involved. Could it be that the Seventh-day Adventist Church, which makes the high profession of being God's remnant church of the last days, has unwittingly inherited a medieval concept of the church from the Roman Catholic Church? Could it be that we have a wrong theology of the church, and that it is this which is crippling God's work in these last days?

Correct theology will result in correct practice. Wrong theology will result in a distorted practice. As long as we fail to return to the biblical concept of the laity and the church, we will continue in Laodicean indifference and fail to see the work of God finished. We say that we believe that the work will be finished by a revived lay movement. If we are ever going to see God's work go forward as it should, we must again make our church a lay person's church. The whole church must become involved in the ministry of the whole church. Pastors need to actively encourage the work of the laity and begin preparing the church for the full ministry of the laity. It is time to call all laity to the aid of the church in fully restoring the ministry of the laity. May we soon see that day.

Notes:

1. Some of the ideas expressed in Chapters 2 and 3 of this book were inspired by the book *Every Believer a Minister*, by Dr. Rex D. Edwards (Boise, Idaho: Pacific Press Publishing Association, 1979). The author wishes to acknowledge this work as helping to challenge him in thinking through this basic New Testament concept and the revolutionary implications it has had for his own ministry.

3

Who Are the Laity?

W ho—indeed—are the laity? Does that appear to be a strange question? Everyone knows who the laity are. Laity are the amateurs, and clergy are the professionals! Such definitions may apply in the secular world, but they are totally foreign to the New Testament concept of the laity.

The term *laity* is derived from the Greek "ho laos." Its basic meaning is "the people of God." Thus anyone who is a part of the people of God is considered laity. By this definition, even clergy are laity. In the previous chapter, we learned that all laity are ministers, but now we will discover that the converse is also true—all ministers are laity.

Ministers do perform ministry, but when they do so, they are acting in the role of the laity—of which they are a vital part. Ministry has been committed to all the people of God and must never become the domain of the privileged few whom we call clergy:

Therefore if any man be in Christ, he is a new creature: old things are passed away; behold, all things are become new. And all things are of God, who hath reconciled us to himself by Jesus Christ, and hath given to us the ministry of reconciliation; To wit, that God was in Christ, reconciling the world unto himself, not imputing their trespasses unto them; and hath committed unto us the word of reconciliation. Now then we are ambassadors for Christ, as though God did beseech you by us; we pray you in Christ's stead, be ye reconciled to God.—2 Corinthians 5:17-20, KJV.

God has reconciled us to Himself through Christ's death on Calvary. Note that it is by virtue of Christ's redemptive ministry that the work of reconciliation has been committed to Christians. To all who have been reconciled has been given the ministry of reconciliation. If all believers have been reconciled, then obviously the work of reconciliation—the work of the ministry—is for all. And if that is true, then it follows logically and biblically that all Christians are ministers.

Laypeople are the front-line soldiers for Christ. Their ministry occurs not in church buildings, but in factories, offices, neighborhoods, and health clubs. In the midst of the normal activities of life, they minister for Christ. That is where real ministry occurs—not in the church building on Sabbath morning. In this sense, "laity" are more "ministers" than clergy.

In the early church, members and leaders were not pew warmers; they were actively engaged in ministry. As one writer has pointed out: "The church does not *have* a ministry, it *is* ministry."[1] Rarely does the world come in contact with the church through the clergy or the theologians of the church. The unchurched person confronts the church through the average member in the neighborhood, at work, or at a social gathering. That is where the world meets the church.

The primary function of the church, then, must be the training of ministers who will in turn meet the world for Christ. The church does not exist for self-perpetuation, but for the enhancement of the ministries of its individual members. Thus, as someone has said: "the church is a mini-seminary, of which the pastor is the dean."

The pastor may function as a leader, a source of inspiration, or an organizer, but the pastor cannot and must not attempt to do the whole work of the ministry, for this is the job of the whole church. However, the pastor does perform a work of ministry, not because he is a pastor, but because he is first of all a lay person, and because that is the work of the laity.

One does not need to be a pastor to give Bible studies. That is ministry and is therefore the work of the laity. One does not need pastoral credentials to visit church members or make hospital calls. That, too, is ministry and is therefore the full domain of the laity.

Whenever a pastor gives Bible studies, visits, makes hospital calls, or carries out any other kind of ministry, he is performing the work of the laity and not the work of the pastor. Clearly, the pastor is not hired to perform ministry. That is not his function but the function of the laity.

However, the pastor does perform ministry—he does give Bible studies, visit, and make hospital calls. Why? Because the pastor is also a lay person, and as a lay person, he must perform his ministry as a part of the people of God. Yet he performs this ministry, not because he is clergy, but because he is first of all a lay person.

Someone may protest that the pastor is supposed to be the shepherd of the flock, and that as a shepherd, he should care for the flock. Yes, the pastor is the shepherd, and yes, he cares for the flock. However, his care does not extend to performing ministry that the flock should be doing for themselves. The shepherd's job is to keep the sheep in shape so that they can produce sheep. If the shepherd is really caring for the flock, he will be training his members for their ministry.

The danger of a clergy-dominated church is that it can lead to the creation of a highly critical congregation. That's why the best remedy for a sick church is to put it to work. As the church goes to work, many of the problems it has will disappear. At times the pastor may have to deal with some severe problems in the church. We are not suggesting that he ignore problems—but that he not major in problems. Many problems will be cared for if clergy will release people into ministry.

It is the professional spectator who becomes the professional critic. Who is always yelling "Kill the umpire"? Who is the "Monday morning quarterback"? The spectator, of course.

"Spectator Christianity ultimately becomes critical, sterile, and unproductive. It observes and criticizes others, but never gets committed into life with Christ."[2] Yet, somehow, in the New Testament sense "the spectator . . . is not a Christian, even though he sits in church."[3] To be a Christian means to be involved—to be engaged in ministry. There can be no Christianity without ministry involvement.

> It is not the critic who counts, pointing out how the strong man stumbled or where the doer of deeds could have done better. The credit belongs to the man who is actually in the arena, whose face is marred by dust and sweat and blood; who strives valiantly, who errs, and comes short again and again, but knows great enthusiasm and great devotion and spends himself. Who at the best knows in the end the triumph of high achievement, in a worthy cause, and who at the worst if he fails, at least fails while doing greatly. So that his place shall never be with those cold and timid souls who know neither victory nor defeat.
> —*Theodore Roosevelt*

The early church had only a few great preachers like Peter, Paul, Apollos, and Barnabas, yet it turned the world upside down. Why? Because it could count on the individual witness of the faithful. We know very little about the founders of most of the early Christian churches. There are no great names. They were founded by laypeople. These anonymous laypeople are the ones who are really responsible for the fantastic growth of the early church. It is in precisely the same way that the church of the last days must finish the work of God—with the power of the ministry of the laity.

The pastor may be the employed minister of the church, who gives his full time to directing the work of the church. Yet the lay person is also a full-time minister for Christ, who performs ministry in his assigned roles as well as representing the church in all of his activities. Please note that the difference between laity and clergy is not that one is full-time and the other is part-time. Both laity and clergy are engaged in full-time ministry because the Christian life is ministry.

Somehow the concept of clergy and laity working together as a team, as they did in New Testament times, must be recaptured if the work is ever to be finished. This church must once again become truly a lay movement. Remember Ellen White's penetrating statement:

> The work of God in the earth can never be finished until the men and women comprising our church membership rally to the work and unite their efforts with those of ministers and church officers. —*Gospel Workers*, pp. 351, 352.

Early Adventism's View of Laity and Clergy

We have seen clearly from the Bible that the role of the laity is in the performance of ministry. It is not the job of the pastor to be the sole minister in the church. In fact, as previously stated, whenever pastors perform ministry, they are doing the work of the laity rather than the work of the pastor. The work of the pastor will be discussed in the next chapter.

Early Adventism, with its heavy biblical emphasis, saw that God had called this church into being to operate on a different plane. We were not to be like other churches that had pastors who performed ministry for the people. The Adventist pastor was to be free of pastoral care generally, and the members were to be taught to care for themselves and not to depend on their pastors.

However, like Israel of old, we did not like being different. We wanted to be like the other churches, whose pastors performed ministry for them. So we decided that we wanted a "king over us" too—a pastor who could care for us. And as with ancient Israel, God allowed it, even though it was totally contrary to His plan for this church.

So we hired our pastors. We, the laity, then sat back and watched the pastors work themselves to death, while we criticized them for not doing it right. Eventually, we were not even satisfied to have a pastor over three or four churches; we each wanted a pastor over our own church. "After all," we cried, "we pay our tithe to the conference. Why shouldn't the conference send us a pastor? We're losing our members because we don't have a pastor!"

Tragically, the above scene has been repeated all over North America. The result has been financially strapped conferences, who don't have enough money to send pastors into new areas to raise up churches. Existing churches many times act like leeches on the funds of the conference, trying to protect their self-interest instead of being concerned about reaching the unreached populations of earth.

If the work of God is going to be finished, we need to return to primitive Adventism's concept of clergy and laity. Churches need to rise up and inform their conferences, "We can care for ourselves. Take the money formerly used to give us a pastor and send our pastor out to raise up a new church, whose believers can likewise be taught to care for themselves."

This may seem revolutionary to some. But the times in which we live demand revolution. We cannot continue the church as we have in the past. The times demand that we fully prepare for the finishing of the work of God with an empowered laity. The above scenario may especially need to happen in small churches with little chance for growth. In some of our larger churches, pastors may be needed, but their job description must change to be in harmony with the biblical counsel, as we shall see in the next chapter.

The reason early Adventism grew so rapidly in North America and was in such a healthy condition was that the laity was totally involved in the work of the church. In an interview with G. B. Starr during a series of evangelistic meetings, the Wabash, Indiana *Plain Dealer* reported on October 1, 1886, (p. 5):

THE SEVENTH DAY ADVENTISTS
Some Facts and Figures Gathered
from Elder Starr—How they
have Grown in Forty
Years—and What
They Believe

"By what means have you carried forward your work so rapidly?"

"Well, in the first place," replied the Elder, "we have no settled pastors. Our churches are taught largely to take care of themselves, while nearly all of our ministers work as evangelists in new fields. In the winter they go out into the churches, halls, or school house and raise up believers. In the summer we use tents, pitching them in the cities and villages where we teach the people these doctrines. This year we shall run about 100 tents in this way. Besides these, we send out large numbers of colporters with our tracts and books, who visit the families and teach them the Bible. Last year we employed about 125 in this manner. Bible reading is another class of

work. The workers go from house to house
holding Bible readings with from one to twenty
individuals. Last year they gave 10,000 of such
Bible readings. At the same time we had
employed about 300 canvassers, constantly
canvassing the country and selling our larger
works. In addition to this every church has a
missionary society. Last year these numbered
10,500 members. Every one of these members
does more or less missionary work, such as selling
books, loaning or giving away tracts, obtaining
subscriptions to our periodicals, visiting families,
looking after the poor, aiding the sick, etc. Last
year they made 102,000 visits, wrote 40,000
letters, obtained 38,700 subscriptions to our
periodicals, distributed 15,500,000 pages of
reading matter and 1,600,000 periodicals."

Is it any wonder that early Adventism grew so rapidly in
North America? At that time, North America was much like
the third world today, where members cared for themselves
and pastors were primarily entering new territory. Early
Adventism was fully in harmony with the biblical role of the
laity. Laity performed ministry, and pastors were free to
evangelize new territory. Adventism in North America grew
with great rapidity as a result. Not only did the church grow,
but the members were healthier and more spiritually alive
because they were involved in ministry. This is New Testament Christianity in action.

Even the Seventh-day Baptists at the turn of the century recognized the reason for the substantial growth of
Seventh-day Adventists compared to Seventh-day Baptists. In an article from the Seventh-day Baptist *Sabbath
Recorder* of December 28, 1908 and reprinted in the
Review and Herald of January 14, 1909, several reasons
were offered for the success of Adventists. One of the
reasons given was this:

All Seventh-day Adventist clergymen are missionaries—not located pastors—and are busy preaching, teaching, and organizing churches the world over.

As late as 1912, this was still the predominant view of the clergy/laity relationship in the Seventh-day Adventist Church. In March of 1912, then General Conference President A.G. Daniells, in an address to a ministerial institute in Los Angeles, California, made this assessment of the present situation and a dire prediction for the future if we altered from the biblical position of laity/clergy relationship:

> We have not settled our ministers over churches as pastors to any large extent. In some of the very large churches we have elected pastors, but as a rule we have held ourselves ready for field service, evangelistic work and our brethren and sisters have held themselves ready to maintain their church services and carry forward their church work without settled pastors. And I hope this will never cease to be the order of affairs in this denomination; for when we cease our forward movement work and begin to settle over our churches, to stay by them, and do their thinking and their praying and their work that is to be done, then our churches will begin to weaken, and to lose their life and spirit, and become paralyzed and fossilized and our work will be on a retreat.

Little did A.G. Daniells realize that his words would be so prophetic. In the decades that followed, the Seventh-day Adventist Church left its biblical roots as to the relationship between laity and clergy. Slowly, we started adding settled pastors over the various churches. The result was quickly seen. The more settled pastors we added, the less we grew. The churches who had their own pastors grew spiritually weaker. Daniells' words accurately describe the Seventh-day Adventist Church in North America today. We are fossilized and paralyzed, and our work is on a retreat! It is time for Seventh-day Adventists in North America to wake up. It is time to return to the early Adventist view of laity and clergy. Perhaps we have come so far away from the ideal that it will prove too difficult to return. But try we must, if we are at all serious about finishing the work of God. Listen to these penetrating words from the pen of inspiration:

> The ministers are hovering over churches, which know the truth, while thousands are perishing out of Christ. If the proper instruction were given, if the proper methods were followed, every church member would do his work as a member of the body. . . . They should be taught that unless they can stand alone, without a minister, they need to be converted anew, and baptized anew. They need to be born again.—*General Conference Bulletin*, April 12, 1901, p. 204.

This indeed sounds like radical thinking. It is. But it is New Testament thinking. Laity and clergy are alike responsible for the present condition of things. Laity asked for pastors to hover over them. Clergy enjoyed the new relationship. And the result is the present situation.

The road back will not be easy. It has taken us decades to depart from God's plan for the laity. It is to be hoped that it will not take us decades to return. But the hour is too late to wait any longer. Let's begin now by at least teaching the biblical concept of the laity and by allowing the clergy to return to their biblical role as described in the next chapter. Remember, if church members cannot be taught to be on their own, without the clergy, then they need to be rebaptized and reconverted. This is a spiritual problem, and Ellen White has clearly directed this church to a new beginning based on a new relationship between laity and clergy.

Let's begin now!

Notes:

1. Henrick Kraemer, *A Theology of the Laity* (Philadelphia: Westminster Press, 1958), p. 137.

2. Rex D. Edwards, *Every Believer a Minister* (Boise, Idaho: Pacific Press Publishing Association, 1979), p. 20.

3. *Ibid.*, p. 21.

4

The Biblical Role of the Pastor

It was Ingathering time at the Anytown Seventh-day Adventist Church. Pastor John had recently arrived as the new pastor of this church of thirty active members. The previous pastor had boasted about the fact that he and his family had raised the entire $800 Ingathering goal by themselves. They had caroled every night between Thanksgiving and Christmas, but they had made it. How proud the church was of their pastor!

But Pastor John was different. He did not believe that it was God's will for the pastor to do all the work of the ministry. So Pastor John announced to the congregation that Ingathering would begin Saturday evening after sundown. He encouraged all the members to come out each night that week so that they could have their goal by the end of the week.

Saturday evening Pastor John arrived at the church early and set up the materials for the members to go caroling. The time announced came and went, and no members showed up. Pastor John waited a whole hour, hoping someone would come. When no one did, he put away the Ingathering supplies and took his family home. The same scenario was repeated every night that week. And every night Pastor John enjoyed an evening with his family.

The next Sabbath, members inquired about Ingathering. Had they raised the goal? They were absolutely astounded when Pastor John announced that not one penny had been raised. "But," they asked, "didn't you go out?" Pastor John replied that he was willing to go out as long as one member showed up, but he should not be expected to raise the full goal. One member became quite disturbed as she cried out, "But pastor, if we don't reach our goal, we cannot have our victory banquet!"

That year they did not raise their Ingathering goal. But the church learned a valuable lesson, and within two years this church led the conference in per capita Ingathering.

Does this story sound far-fetched? It actually happened. And I'm fearful that the early attitude of the Anytown Church is being repeated in many Adventist churches. We expect the pastor to perform all the ministry of the church. As we learned in the previous chapter, that is not God's plan for the church.

Some of you who are pastors may be wondering about now, "What is my job?" Throughout your ministry, you have thought that you were supposed to be the minister of the church. If you don't give all the Bible studies and care for all the visiting, what will you do? Will you be out of a job? No, you will be free to do the job assigned to you by God!

The Pastor's Job

In listing the spiritual gifts in Ephesians 4, the apostle Paul delineates one of those gifts as being that of a pastor. In fact, in Ephesians 4 Paul is primarily talking about the "people gifts" that God has given the church. These gifts include apostles, prophets, evangelists, pastors, and teachers. These gifts are given for a specific purpose. They are all basically clergy gifts. Note Paul's assessment of their role:

> And he gave some, apostles; and some prophets; and some, evangelists; and some pastors and teachers; For the perfecting of the saints, for the work of the ministry, for the edifying of the body of Christ: Till we all come in the unity of the faith, and of the knowledge of the Son of God, unto a perfect man, unto the measure of the stature of the fullness of Christ.—Ephesians 4:11-13, KJV.

Here, then, are the people gifts that have been given to the church. Verse 13 indicates that these gifts are to endure until we reach the unity of the faith, which will be at the second coming of Christ. These clergy gifts are always going to be needed. Verse 12 indicates the purpose of these gifts. According to the King James Version, it appears that these gifts are for the perfecting of the saints, for the work of the ministry, and for the edifying of the body of Christ.

However, a misplaced comma in this text in the King James Version creates serious consequences for our theology of the layperson and the pastor. If the King James Version is correct in placing a comma in verse 12 after "saints," then it would be possible to interpret the text to indicate that one of the jobs of the pastor is the work of the ministry. Yet we have clearly seen that the work of the ministry belongs to the laity, not to the pastor.

All modern versions of this text translate it far more accurately by eliminating the comma, which would make it read: "for the perfecting of the saints for the work of the ministry." In other words, the role of the pastor would be to perfect the saints for their ministry. This text is not describing the pastor as a performer of ministry, but instead as a trainer of ministers. Note other translations of this text:[1]

> To fit His people for the work of the

ministry.—*Twentieth Century New Testament.*[2]

In order fully to equip His people for the work of serving.—*Weymouth.*[3]

For the immediate equipment of God's people for the work of service.—*Williams.*[4]

To equip God's people for work in His service.—*New English Bible.*[5]

In order to get His holy people ready to serve as workers.—*Beck.*[6]

His gifts were made that Christians might be properly equipped for their service.—*Phillips.*[7]

All of these translations make abundantly clear that the biblical job description of the pastor is of one who trains and equips members for their ministry. The New Testament views clergy, not as performers of ministry, but as trainers of people for their ministries. This is the primary function of the New Testament pastor.

The work of the pastor is to prepare God's people to do the work of the ministry. It is not the job of the pastor to be the only soul winner in the church. It is not the job of the pastor to do the work of the ministry, but to train the members to do the work of the ministry. It is true that the pastor, as stated in the previous chapter, performs ministry. He does give Bible studies, counsel, visit, etc. But whenever he does it, he is acting in the capacity of a layperson and is not functioning as a pastor. What the pastor is paid to do is to train the members. If he is not doing that, then biblically, he is not doing his job.

The Pastor As Trainer

Not only does the Bible mandate training as the chief function of the pastor, but Ellen White does, as well:

> Let the minister devote more of his time to
> educating than to preaching. Let him teach the
> people how to give to others the knowledge they
> have received. —*Testimonies for the Church*, vol.
> 7, p. 20.

Most pastors would consider preaching to be their chief function. Many laity would likewise concur. While not minimizing the importance of preaching and the great need for strong, biblical preaching in the Adventist church, Ellen White states emphatically that the teaching or equipping role of the pastor should take more time than the preaching role. Yet most pastors spend far more time preparing and preaching sermons than on teaching members how to perform their ministry.

> It is not the Lord's purpose that ministers
> should be left to do the greatest part of the work
> of sowing the seeds of truth. —*Ibid.*, p. 21.

In most Adventist churches, this counsel is not followed today. If the pastor does not do it, it doesn't get done. Why shouldn't pastors do all the seed sowing? Because seed sowing is ministry—and ministry is the job of the laity. Ellen White again states emphatically that the pastor's first job is to train the members, even before reaching unbelievers.

> In laboring where there are already some in
> the faith, the minister should at first seek not so
> much to convert unbelievers, as to train the
> church members for acceptable
> co-operation. —*Gospel Workers*, p. 196.

When the pastor takes over the ministry function of the church and neglects the training function, the church becomes weak spiritually. There is a definite connection between how pastors govern the church and the spirituality of

the church. Any pastor who spends most of his time ministering to the members will create a church that is weak
spiritually, while conversely, a pastor who spends most of
his time training and equipping his members will create a
church that is much stronger spiritually.

> God has not given His ministers the work of
> setting the churches right. No sooner is this work
> done apparently, than it has to be done over again.
> Church members that are thus looked after and
> labored for become religious weaklings. If nine
> tenths of the effort that has been put forth for
> those who know the truth had been put forth for
> those who have never heard the truth, how much
> greater would have been the advancement
> made!—*Testimonies for the Church*, vol. 7, p. 18.

Nurture for the sake of nurture produces religious weaklings, states the servant of the Lord. Some pastors feel they
must nurture people first. Then these nurtured people will
automatically go out and witness. However, that is completely contrary to the counsel. Ellen White's view is that
this methodology produces religious weaklings—
Laodiceans. Since this is what most pastors have been doing,
is it any wonder that our churches are full of religious
weaklings? The more care we give them, the weaker they
become spiritually.

The great danger churches face as they mature is to
spend time tending the aquarium of the saints rather than
becoming fishers of men. Yet strangely, the more time they
spend nurturing the saints, the weaker the saints become.
Even the New Testament church was in danger of losing
this sense of mission in its embryonic years. The danger was
that the church would stop its forward movement and
center on strengthening the saints in Jerusalem. To prevent
this, God allowed persecution to come to the Jerusalem
believers so that they would be scattered and thus be forced
to concentrate on mission for their own spiritual strength.

> Forgetting that strength to resist evil is best
> gained by aggressive service, they began to think
> that they had no work so important as that of
> shielding the church in Jerusalem from the attacks
> of the enemy. Instead of educating the new
> converts to carry the gospel to those who had not
> heard it, they were in danger of taking a course
> that would lead all to be satisfied with what had
> been accomplished. To scatter His representatives
> abroad, where they could work for others, God
> permitted persecution to come upon them.
> Driven from Jerusalem, the believers "went
> everywhere preaching the word."—Ellen G.
> White, *The Acts of the Apostles*, p. 105.

"Strength to resist evil is best gained by aggressive service." This is the way to victory. The best method by which people can be nurtured and gain victory in their personal lives is by working for souls. So states the pen of inspiration.

> Those who would be overcomers must be
> drawn out of themselves; and the only thing which
> will accomplish this great work, is to become
> intensely interested in the salvation of
> others.—Ellen G. White, *Fundamentals of
> Christian Education*, p. 207.

It is impossible to be nurtured apart from involvement in soul winning. Ellen White is crystal clear: the only way out of Laodicean lukewarmness is to become involved in evangelistic ministry.

Dr. Kenneth Van Wyk, pastor of the Garden Grove (California) Community Church and a modern church growth expert, confirms what Ellen White told this church nearly one hundred years ago.

> In my judgment, nurture-oriented education
> commits the serious error of making an end out of

something that is meant to be a means. By definition it is self-centered and therefore suffers from basic introversion. . . . The mission-oriented Christian education program holds that the primary purpose of education is to equip people for the growth and outreach of the church. . . . The church is a training center where the people of God are equipped for their respective areas of ministry and mission. Nurture, indeed, comes as a by-product of being equipped and involved in ministry. My experience in Christian education is that a mission mentality in the church motivates people to training and produces astounding results in personal spiritual growth as well as church growth. —*Pastor's Church Growth Handbook*, vol. 1, p. 134.

Training is the best nurture that can be given to God's people, but nurture for the sake of nurture only embeds people more deeply into Laodicean indifference. Our churches have been nurtured to death. We don't need more nurture. We need training for mission. Training and involving people in ministry is the best nurture we can give them. It is precisely because people have not been trained and involved in ministry that we have so much need of nurture in the church today.

The best remedy for Laodicea is not preaching about Laodicea, it is not preaching about the sins of the church, it is not telling people they ought to go to work. The best remedy for Laodicea is for pastors to train members and then put them into meaningful ministry in harmony with their spiritual gifts. (Setting up a gift-based training program in the local church will be discussed later in this book.)

> Sometimes ministers do too much; they seek to embrace the whole work in their arms. It absorbs and dwarfs them; yet they continue to grasp it all. They seem to think that they alone are to work in the cause of God, while the members of the

church stand idle. This is not God's order at
all.—*Evangelism*, p. 113.

The greatest help that can be given our people
is to teach them to work for God, and to depend
on Him, not on the ministers.—*Testimonies for
the Church*, vol. 7, p. 19.

So long as church members make no effort to
give others the help given them, great spiritual
feebleness must result.—*Ibid.*, pp. 18, 19.

The counsel that Ellen White has given the Seventh-day
Adventist church is abundantly clear. Ellen White viewed
the role of Adventist ministers as completely different from
the traditional pastoral role of the nineteenth century. She
was one hundred years ahead of her time.

Today most church growth authorities state that the role
of the pastor must be that of a trainer/equipper. Yet Adventists have a mandate from their prophet for the pastor to be
the trainer! How can we continue to create Laodicea by
refusing to return to the biblical role of the pastor as the
trainer and equipper of the laity for their ministry?

So strong is the counsel that God has given this church
in this regard that Ellen White even intimates that any
pastor who is performing ministry instead of training his
members for ministry should be fired. That sounds harsh,
but she says it.

In some respects the pastor occupies a position
similar to that of the foreman of a gang of laboring
men or the captain of a ship's crew. They are
expected to see that the men over whom they are
set, do the work assigned to them correctly and
promptly, and only in case of emergency are they
to execute in detail.

The owner of a large mill once found his
superintendent in a wheel-pit, making some

simple repairs, while a half-dozen workmen in the line were standing by, idly looking on. The proprietor, after learning the facts, so as to be sure that no injustice was done, called the foreman to his office and handed him his discharge with full pay. In surprise the foreman asked for an explanation. It was given in these words: "I employed you to keep six men at work. I found the six idle, and you doing the work of but one. Your work could have been done just as well by any one of the six. I cannot afford to pay the wages of seven for you to teach the six how to be idle."

This incident may be applicable in some cases, and in others not. But many pastors fail in not knowing how or in not trying, to get the full membership of the church actively engaged in the various departments of church work. If pastors would give more attention to getting and keeping their flock actively engaged at work, they would accomplish more good, have more time for study and religious visiting, and also avoid many causes of friction.—*Gospel Workers*, pp. 197, 198.

Does that statement blow your mind? Remember the statement from A. G. Daniells, quoted in the last chapter? He knew the counsel of the Lord for the Adventist ministry. He had learned it first-hand from Ellen White. He knew that if we departed from the counsel, our churches would fossilize. No wonder he warned us. But Ellen White warns us even more so. What would happen if conference presidents followed this counsel? There would be few of us pastors left.

This is not meant to be an indictment of the Adventist ministry. We have only performed as we have been taught. Let not the laity cast blame at the pastors, and let not the pastors blame the laity. We got into this problem together. We need to resolve it together. Rather than casting stones at each other, let us come to God and beg His forgiveness for our failure to follow His guidance. Then, under the direction of the Holy Spirit, let laypeople and pastors get together and find a solution to our present problem. It's time to get out of Laodicea. It's time for the laity to resume their role as the performers of ministry. It's time for the pastors to shoulder their role as trainers of the laity. Let's start following the counsel God has given us!

It needs to be clearly stated that we cannot accomplish a return to the biblical model overnight. Pastors cannot immediately stop caring for the flock and expect the churches to survive—they would probably die. We have created a dependency that can only be relieved as members are trained to care for the flock. As they are trained, then the pastor can be released a little at a time. Even if we are unable to come all the way back to the biblical ideal, at least we should begin moving in that direction. The first step will be getting the laity and their pastors together to discuss the problem. Hopefully, we can do so without being judgmental or protective of turf, but with a genuine desire to bring our churches back into line with God's ideal.

Results of Lay Ministry in the Local Church

What would our churches be like if they were modeled after the divine ideal? In Ephesians 4, after informing us of the purpose of the clergy gifts, the apostle Paul describes what the church is like when the clergy spiritual gifts are used as God intended:

> Till we all come in the unity of the faith, and of the knowledge of the Son of God, unto a perfect man, unto the measure of the stature of the fullness of Christ.—Ephesians 4:12, 13, KJV.

One of the great benefits of a lay ministry program established on spiritual gifts operating in the church is unity. One of the crying needs of Adventist churches today is unity. The biblical prescription to bring about unity is the utilization of the clergy gifts as trainers and equippers, putting God's people to work:

> That we henceforth be no more children,
> tossed to and fro, and carried about with every
> wind of doctrine, by the sleight of men, and
> cunning craftiness, whereby they lie in wait to
> deceive: but speaking the truth in love, may grow
> up into him in all things, which is the head, even
> Christ. —Ephesians 4:14, 15, KJV.

The object of the spiritual gifts is not only unity, but maturity. The proper use of the gifts causes believers to be less childish. Scripture indicates, as Ellen White confirms, that nurture of the saints occurs as a result of being properly equipped for ministry.

One of the problems of contemporary Adventism is that members no longer seem to be firmly grounded in the faith. Adventists don't know their Bibles as they used to; they are easily swayed by false doctrines and get caught up in all kinds of aberrant movements. Paul indicates that one of the blessings of a lay ministry based on spiritual gifts is that members are no longer "tossed to and fro, and carried about by every wind of doctrine." The reason is that when people are actively involved in working for others, they grow spiritually, and it forces them into a regular program of Bible study and prayer. It is difficult for false doctrine to take hold of a church that is actively reaching out in ministry to the lost.

> From whom the whole body fitly joined
> together and compacted by that which every joint
> supplieth, according to the effectual working in
> the measure of every part, maketh increase of the
> body unto the edifying of itself in love.
> —Ephesians 4:16, KJV.

Here Paul likens the church to the human body with all

its joints, fitting perfectly together to accomplish the tasks of the body. In the hand alone there are fourteen joints, excluding the wrist, yet all joints work smoothly in harmony. If one joint doesn't work correctly, the hand ceases to function properly. So it is with the spiritual body; all the members need to work smoothly together.

The joints in the body don't just start working together, however. A little child has a hard time getting his joints to work together so that he can walk, yet by persistent trying, he eventually learns. As the child grows, the joints automatically work together; he doesn't even have to think about it. Learning, however, can sometimes be a painful thing. The child falls, bruises his legs, and cries. Yet the child learns in spite of his mistakes and bruises. So it will be with the church. There may be bruises as we learn to work together, but if we don't try, we will never accomplish anything for the Lord.

What is a joint? A joint is the coming together of two or more different bones so that they work together as one. Bone troubles usually develop at these points of contact. Within the body, joints are a danger, yet they are a vital necessity. The church is like that. An individual Christian, if he remains all by himself, does not create any friction, but he does not contribute anything positive to the church. It is in connection with other people that we grow and contribute to the church. We need each other. The health and growth of the church family depend on our working harmoniously together.

Joints are the source of a myriad of possible diseases and disfigurements. They are also the only means by which we can walk, eat, sing, or kneel to pray. The reason for unity in a diversity of gifts displayed in the church is that all are "fitly joined" to the Head, which is Christ. Thus persons of varying gifts are able to work together. Every part has its essential function to perform. Every member becomes a working member. This is the only way in which the church can fulfill God's plan.

What are the results, then, of this spiritual gifts, lay

ministry program operating in the local church? What happens when the pastor becomes the trainer and the equipper and the members fulfill their role by becoming involved in ministry in harmony with their spiritual gifts? There are two results: first, the growth of the church in numbers, and second, a growth of individuals in spiritual maturity. May God perform both works as we realign our churches in harmony with the biblical ideal.

Notes:

1. The following six scripture references are as published in *The Word: The Bible From 26 Translations*. Reprinted by permission of Mathis Publishers, Inc. Box 8621, Moss Point, MS 39563.

2. From *The Twentieth Century New Testament*. Moody Bible Institute. Reprinted by permission.

3. From *Weymouth's New Testament in Modern Speech*, by Richard Francis Weymouth, as revised by J.A. Robertson. Published by special arrangement with James Clarke and Company, Ltd., London. Reprinted by permission of Harper and Row Publishers, Inc., and James Clarke and Company, Ltd.

4. From *The New Testament: A Translation in the Language of the People,* by Charles B. Williams. Copyright © 1937 by Bruce Humphries, Inc. Copyright © renewed 1965 by Edith S. Williams. Reprinted by permission.

5. From *The New English Bible: New Testament*. Copyright © 1961 by The Delegates of the Oxford University Press and The Syndics of the Cambridge University Press. Reprinted by permission.

6. From *The New Testament in the Language of Today*, by William F. Beck. Copyright © 1963 by Concordia Publishing House. Reprinted by permission.

7. From *The New Testament in Modern English*. Copyright © 1958, 1959, 1960 by J.B. Phillips. Published by MacMillan Publishing Company, a division of MacMillan, Inc. Reprinted by permission. Reprinted for distribution in Canada by permission of Fount, an imprint of HarperCollins Publishers, Ltd.

5

Who Needs
Spiritual Gifts?

Have you ever been asked to fill a position in the church for which you didn't feel qualified, and yet you were pressured into accepting the role anyway? As a result of people being persuaded to serve the church in areas where they are not gifted, many have become disillusioned and refuse to become involved in church activities any longer. That's why it is so critical to have a gift-based ministry operating in the local church. If we are serious about lay involvement, we must take the time to help people discover their spiritual gifts and find their place of ministry in the church.

Spiritual gifts, however, have had a stormy history in the church. This probably has been due to the all too prevalent misuse of these gifts in the Christian church. In fact, the spiritual gifts issue was one of the first major controversies to erupt in the Christian church at Corinth.

Spiritual gifts have also had a stormy history in the

Adventist church. Many Adventists have been fearful of a spiritual gifts emphasis because of how the gift of tongues has been misused in Pentecostal groups. We must not allow the fact that there is a counterfeit, however, to destroy the blessing of the genuine spiritual gifts God has poured out upon His church.

Adventists, from their inception, have been believers in spiritual gifts. Sometimes, tragically, they have been as guilty as the Pentecostals in elevating one gift over all others—the gift of prophecy. While the prophetic gift is valuable, essential, and genuine, we must not limit spiritual gifts to the gift of prophecy alone. All the gifts of the Spirit must be manifested in the church.

In other chapters we will examine the logistics of setting up a gift-based ministry in the local church. In this chapter, however, we wish to examine the biblical basis for the doctrine of spiritual gifts. It is our purpose to show that discovering and utilizing our spiritual gifts is a vital part of our preparation for the second coming of Jesus. Thus, the teaching of a spiritual gifts ministry is a unique Adventist doctrine. This was the view of Ellen White, as noted in the following statements:

> God has set in the church different gifts. These are precious in their proper places, and all may act a part in the work of preparing a people for Christ's soon coming.—*Gospel Workers*, p. 481.

> Sermons have been in great demand in our churches. The members have depended upon pulpit declamations instead of on the Holy Spirit. Uncalled for and unused, the spiritual gifts bestowed on them have dwindled into feebleness.—*Selected Messages*, book 1, p. 127.

> Ministers frequently neglect these important branches of the work—health reform, spiritual gifts, systematic benevolence, and the great

branches of the missionary work. Under their labors large numbers may embrace the theory of the truth, but in time it is found that there are many who will not bear the proving of God.—*Evangelism*, p. 256.

We have certainly spent more time on health reform than on spiritual gifts. Not that health reform should be neglected; it should not. Yet we have whole departments of the church to deal with health reform, while very few in our churches have been educated about spiritual gifts. Spiritual gifts is one of the most neglected subjects in Adventism.

Remember Ellen White's statement, quoted in a previous chapter, about the work never being finished until laity and clergy team together? Now the servant of the Lord tells us that we have neglected teaching spiritual gifts to our people, and therefore they are not prepared for Christ's coming. Could there be a connection, then, between advent preparation, spiritual gifts, and the ministry of laity who have been trained by their pastors?

I believe that this is the thrust of the statements from Ellen White that we have examined. It is also the reason we need desperately to develop a gift-based ministry in our churches.

The Parable of the Talents

Not only has Ellen White stressed our need to discover our spiritual gifts as a part of our preparation for Christ's coming, but Jesus Himself makes this connection in the parable of the talents recorded in Matthew 25:14-30. Jesus was nearing the end of His ministry; crucifixion time was near. He was anxious for His disciples, and in Matthew 24 He unburdened Himself to them concerning the future. Matthew 24 is recognized as Jesus' great sermon on the second coming. But the sermon doesn't just end with the signs of His coming. Jesus quickly followed the signs with two parables—the parable of the ten virgins and the parable of the talents. Both deal with preparation for His coming.

The parable of the virgins ends with an injunction to watch. The parable of the talents tells how the virgins should have been watching. The parable of the virgins stresses our need for the oil of the Holy Spirit in order to be ready for the coming of Christ. The parable of the talents reveals that God, through the Holy Spirit, is the dispenser of the gifts or talents that enable His people to work for Him.

When Christians receive the Holy Spirit, they utilize the gifts that the Holy Spirit gives them. The point of these parables is that the watching time is not to be spent in idle waiting, but in diligent working. Thus the parable of the virgins teaches personal preparation for the Advent, while the parable of the talents indicates that there is a work to be done to prepare others for the Advent. The virgins point to the inward spiritual life of the faithful; the talents describe their external activity.

What the Parable Teaches About Spiritual Gifts

Eight lessons can be learned from studying the parable of the talents:

1. The talents represent spiritual gifts.

While the talents in the parable referred originally to money given to each of the servants, they are also symbols of the spiritual gifts God has bestowed upon His church.

> All men do not receive the same gifts, but to every servant of the Master some gift of the Spirit is promised. —*Christ's Object Lessons*, p. 327.

2. The gift of talents is the prerogative of God.

Spiritual gifts do not originate with people. They come from God. In the parable, the husbandman—God—is seen as the dispenser of the gifts. It is He who decides who gets what gifts and how many.

> Again, it will be like a man going on a journey,

who called his servants and entrusted his property
to them. — Matthew 25:14, NIV.

The gifts (or property) do not belong to people — they
belong to God. They are His gifts, and they have only been
entrusted to His servants. Spiritual gifts do not refer to the
natural talents all of us receive through our genes, but to
special gifts bestowed upon believers through the Holy
Spirit.

Yet for the believer, becoming a Christian means a com-
plete surrender of the life to Christ, including natural talents
and abilities. When we come to Christ, we give Him everything. He then returns even these natural talents to us,
embellished by the Holy Spirit. In that sense, even our
natural talents can become spiritual gifts. However, in addition to these natural gifts, God bestows on all believers
unique spiritual gifts to be used in ministry for the Master.
Since these gifts belong to Christ, we cannot afford to
misuse them. To misuse even one talent shows that we
despise the gifts of Heaven.

In His wisdom, God gives us just the right gifts — no
more, no less. Never bemoan the size of your gift. If God
has not given you first place; then glory in second or third
place. We cannot grumble or be resentful or jealous toward
people with five or two gifts, if we only have one. God has
given us what we can use. He has promised that if we use
the gift we have, He will increase it. The point of the parable
is that we should use our gifts, whatever they are. It's far
better to have last place in God's service with faithfulness
than first place with unfaithfulness.

Remember, no matter how few gifts we have, the command of Christ is to put them to use. The question asked in
the parable is not "How much do you have?" but "What are
you doing with what you have?"

3. Those who use their gifts will receive more. Talents used become talents multiplied.

One of the points of the parable is that those who used

their gifts were given more; those who failed to use their gifts lost what they had. The Lord expects us to utilize our gifts. The reward for the faithful use of one's gifts is the reception of more gifts and more opportunities for service.

The husbandman in the parable does not tell the servants how to use the gifts. He distributes the gifts and leaves their use to the ingenuity of the individual. Mistakes have been made by some in attempting to instigate a spiritual gift-based ministry by arbitrarily assigning people to certain roles based on their perceived gifts. Instead of allowing people to discover—through prayer, meditation, and guidance—the ways God wants them to use their gifts, some church leaders have listed the kinds of ministries people can exercise if they have certain gifts. Such attempts have been well meaning, but usually destroy a gift-based ministry.

People need to decide for themselves how they are going to use their gifts. Church leaders may give counsel, but the process of gift discovery must not be structured to the point of insisting that people utilize their gifts only in certain ways. God may have gifted people so that they will be able to help a church break out of its mold. We must not stifle creativity by insisting that people use their gifts only in the armor we have provided for them.

Some have suggested that because people have the gift of hospitality, they should work in outreach ministry, or that if people have the gift of leadership, they need to work in nurture ministry. I am suggesting that it is possible to use every gift in either outreach or nurture, and the church must be careful that it does not limit people. Let people decide for themselves.

4. Everyone receives some gift.

The Master, as distributor of the gifts, has given some five, some two, and some one. But each servant received at least one gift. The unequal distribution of the talents indicates that each person received what he could use—no more, no less. Therefore there is no such thing as a Christian who does not have at least one gift to use in the Master's service. No one can claim that there is nothing for him or her to do. That's why all members are called into ministry and gifted by God to do something.

5. A talent is valuable.

Some feel that since they only have one gift, it isn't much—so they do nothing. That was the problem with the unfaithful servant. He did not squander his talent; he simply hid it and did nothing with it. Many believers feel that since they have only one gift, they don't have much to offer, but we must realize that each gift is precious because it is God's.

A talent of silver in Bible times was worth twenty years' wages for the common laborer. Today that would equal around a half million dollars. That is not cheap. What God has given each individual in his or her spiritual gift is of tremendous value to God and to the church. People cannot feel unimportant in God's work as long as they are utilizing their spiritual gifts.

6. Utilizing talents means taking risks.

The person who took risks received the greatest commendation in the parable. The servant could have lost everything. So it must be with believers today as they utilize their gifts; they must launch out in faith. Those in the Bible who were the greatest servants of God assumed the greatest risk of failure, loss, and shame—they were people who virtually became laughingstocks among men. Abraham, Moses, Paul, and Peter all took great risks to advance the cause of God, as did the pioneers of Adventism—people such as James and Ellen White. The local church today needs people willing to take risks to advance the work. To use one's gifts means to risk failure; but to fail to use one's gifts *is* failure.

7. Those who fail to use what is given them lose what they have.

The unfaithful servant had the ability to double his one talent. The husbandman expected him to do so. "Thou oughtest" (v. 27) indicates clearly that the man should have used his talent.

The whole parable seems to focus on the one-talent person. Why? Because it is the person with one talent who is most apt to do nothing. The reason the church is not advancing as it should today is not due so much to the multi-gifted people as to the many one-talent people who are doing nothing because they don't think they have much. Christ wants the people with the smallest gifts to understand that they are very valuable in His sight. Their gifts are needed desperately by the church.

8. Those who use their spiritual gifts are preparing to enter heaven; those who don't, suffer an eternal loss.

Utilizing one's spiritual gifts is part of a Christian's preparation for eternity. Failure to utilize one's gifts results in eternal consequences. This is serious business.

> For all the knowledge and ability we might
> have gained and did not, there will be an eternal
> loss. —*Christ's Object Lessons*, p. 363.

The talent was taken away from the unprofitable servant, and he was sent into outer darkness. If Christ had been more graphic, He might have said the servant went straight to "hell." Such are the serious consequences of failing to utilize the gifts bestowed upon the followers of Christ.

The disobedience of the unprofitable servant was not active, but passive. Like many today, he was not actively disobeying his Master, but his failure to do something positive resulted in disobedience.

> Many who excuse themselves from Christian
> effort plead their inability for the work. But did
> God make them so incapable? No, never. This

inability has been produced by their own inactivity and perpetuated by their deliberate choice. Already, in their own characters, they are realizing the result of the sentence, "Take the talent from him." The continual misuse of their talents will effectually quench for them the Holy Spirit, which is the only light. The sentence, "Cast ye the unprofitable servant into outer darkness," sets Heaven's seal to the choice which they themselves have made for eternity.—*Christ's Object Lessons*, p. 365.

This is the terrible indictment of those who fail to utilize their spiritual gifts. We, as Adventists preparing for the coming of our Lord, cannot afford to ignore the doctrine of spiritual gifts, for it is part of our preparation for eternity. The failure to use our gifts, we are told, results in rejection of the Holy Spirit, our only light.

As someone has suggested, the sin of sins in Christ's service is to try to preserve and safeguard the gift which we have been given, so that on demand it can be produced exactly as it was. It's time to start utilizing our spiritual gifts.

Spiritual Gifts and the Early Church

The outpouring of the Holy Spirit on the day of Pentecost resulted in an incredible display of spiritual gifts. As a result, throughout the book of Acts we read of the astounding success of the early church, which took the gospel to the then-known world in thirty years.

Yet there is no theological treatise on spiritual gifts in the book of Acts. Instead, we find a practical implementation of the doctrine of spiritual gifts—we see spiritual gifts in action. The Holy Spirit enables one to preach, another to teach, someone else to be hospitable. In one chapter, we see the Spirit prompting a member to be helpful, in the next to exhort, and in the following chapter to provide capable leadership.

In the organizational phase of the early church, we discover more detailed references to the gifts. In fact, it is over the issue of misused spiritual gifts in the Corinthian church that we have the first formal theological treatise on the subject. The Corinthian problem stemmed from the fact that everyone was coveting the same gift—one they felt was higher than the others. This resulted in spiritual pride as they demonstrated their superior use of the gift of tongues.

Paul's response was to reverse the hierarchy that the Corinthian church had constructed (1 Corinthians 12:28-31). He tried to convey to the disciples in Corinth the deeper truth that the gifts were on a horizontal plane with each other, rather than in a vertical line, and that consequently there really are no "top" gifts and thus no "superior" Christians. As long as people utilize their gifts, they are considered faithful.

Furthermore, Paul indicates that spiritual gifts are not the "sign" that one has received the Spirit. The sign of Spirit baptism is the fruit of the Spirit, especially demonstrated in the lives of loving and lovable Christians. That's why 1 Corinthians 13 appears in the midst of this discussion of spiritual gifts. The gifts are given for the ministry of the saints; the fruit is given for a demonstration of godliness. The Christian needs both and must utilize both, but must also put each in its proper place.

Amazingly, the doctrine of spiritual gifts seems to be one of the first which the devil was able to distort in the early church. That which was responsible for the tremendous explosion of growth in the early church received the first attack of Satan. Obviously, Satan knows that when the church fully understands and implements a spiritual gift ministry, it experiences both internal and external growth, and his kingdom is jeopardized. Therefore, he does all within his power to keep Seventh-day Adventists today from implementing a gift-based ministry in their churches. Satan well knows that when we do this, we will receive the outpouring of the Holy Spirit in latter-rain power, and Christ will come.

There are three basic theological treatises on spiritual gifts in the New Testament: Romans 12, 1 Corinthians 12-14, and Ephesians 4. In all three passages, spiritual gifts always appear as part of the body (the church).

Three approaches are utilized today by churches in developing a gift-based ministry. The first is that all gifts are given to the body; therefore evangelism is a by-product of the body being nurtured through the utilization of the gifts. The problem with this approach is that it lacks intentional planning for witness and results in a self-serving attitude in the church.

The second approach declares that some gifts have been given to the body and that some gifts work through the body to the outside community. If the outreach gift has not been bestowed, then evangelism is not required. The outcome of this approach is that evangelism is viewed as a gift of the few rather than the responsibility of the many.

The third approach, advocated in this book, recognizes that all gifts are given to the body, and that all gifts minister through the body. It allows people to be involved in meaningful ministry both to the body and through the body to the community, without neglecting their spiritual gifts. It is left up to individuals to decide if God is calling them to use their gifts in the body or through the body.

Not only do all gifts work in the body or through the body—they all work to increase the unity of the church. In all three passages that teach spiritual gifts, the unity of the church is discussed as one of the practical benefits of a gift-based ministry. In this sense, every member has been fitted into the body, according to God's master plan, and has been given one or more spiritual gifts to fulfill that function properly. What a delight for people to realize that God has put them into their local church at a particular time because their gifts are needed. If they do not utilize their gift, the church will not be as successful. Every individual is therefore vitally important to develop God's full mosaic in the church.

The second approach to spiritual gifts, just mentioned, sometimes leads to a confusing of gifts and roles. With every gift, there is a corresponding role that each Christian is to fill. For example, not every Christian is given the spiritual gift of evangelism, yet every Christian is still a witness. The gift of evangelism enables a person to effectively reach other people for Christ. It enables him or her to do it better than those who do not have this gift. While not all have this God-gifted ability, all can and should witness, under the blessing of God, to people they come in contact with regularly.

There are times when people must minister even if they don't have the specific gift needed. If someone is hungry, one doesn't refer them to Sister Jones, who has the gift of mercy or hospitality. A Christian feeds the hungry person even if that Christian doesn't have the gift. Therefore, whenever necessary, we will fill the roles present in all of the gifts, even as we exercise the roles called for by our own specific gifts. There will be times when we will be called upon to do things outside of our giftedness. Yet, our major ministry should be in the area of our giftedness.

Spiritual gifts have caused immense problems throughout the history of the church, but they have also been a source of tremendous blessing when properly used. The effectiveness of God's church is directly related to its ability to set up a gift-based ministry in local congregations. It is well worth the time and effort required to institute a gift-based ministry in your church. Why not determine to begin right now?

6

How to Discover Your Spiritual Gifts

Since each believer has at least one gift of the Spirit, all can engage in a search to discover their gifts. As soon as people are baptized, they should be encouraged to enter the process of gift discovery so that they can find a ministry which will utilize their giftedness.

People who have the more "spectacular" gifts would know it very quickly, without much exploration. However, most of us have not been endowed with such gifts. Yet we should expect that they will appear in the church. Ellen White indicates that as we near the end, miracles, signs, and wonders will once again become the order of the day. So the miraculous gifts will reappear. We must be cautious that we don't reject them.

Most of us have received the non-miraculous gifts of the Spirit mentioned in Scripture. For us, there is a process of discovery we should go through to discover which gifts of the Spirit God has bestowed upon us. Having discovered our gifts, we will then need to explore ways in which they can be used in a gift-based ministry. That will be the subject of Chapter 8. When we discover what gifts we have, we will know also what gifts we don't have. This knowledge is important because nothing is more frustrating than trying to do something for which one is not gifted.

The process of discovering our spiritual gifts never ends. We need to keep experimenting to discover our gifts. The parable of the talents teaches that if people use their gifts, more gifts will be given. Therefore, gifts that do not appear today may emerge five years from now. So keep on discovering.

Following are five steps in the discovery process:

1. Pray.

Since spiritual gifts come from the Spirit, they must be discovered in a spiritual context. This should not be just a cursory prayer asking God to reveal what gift the Holy Spirit has given you, but a time of intense prayer, asking God to reveal His will for your ministry. It would be well, as you review the various gifts mentioned in Scripture, to ask God specifically if He has given you that particular gift.

People should not only pray, but also listen to God as He speaks. Some gifts might seem frightening at first, but we should pray that God will make known His will for our spiritual lives. Remember that spiritual things are spiritually discerned. It is impossible to rightly discover our spiritual gifts and find a gift-based ministry without much prayer and searching of heart. Yet the rewards of this time spent with God give the satisfaction of knowing that God's will is being done with the gift that He has given. Nothing will encourage the heart as will the experience of knowing we are where God wants us to be and are utilizing the gifts He has entrusted to us.

2. Explore the possibilities.

We must first of all become familiar with the various gifts that are available. The best place to begin is with the gifts mentioned in Scripture. As we've noted earlier, the three major passages that list the spiritual gifts are Romans 12, 1 Corinthians 12, and Ephesians 4. However, that does not mean that gifts must be limited to the ones mentioned in Scripture. These are suggestive of the gifts that were needed in the first-century church. These were the gifts needed then to propel the church into the tremendous growth that it experienced.

However, we no longer live in the first century; we are moving into the twenty-first century. Gifts needed today to expand God's work may be different from or in addition to the gifts needed in the first century. The Holy Spirit is not limited. He can continually dispense new gifts as they are needed to further the cause of God. While we need to begin with the Scriptural gifts, we must not limit the Holy Spirit nor our exploration to only those mentioned there.

The first listing of spiritual gifts is found in Romans 12:6-8, where seven gifts of the Spirit are mentioned: prophecy, ministry, teaching, exhortation, giving, ruling, and mercy. First Corinthians 12:8-10 mentions nine gifts: wisdom, knowledge, faith, healing, working of miracles, prophecy, discerning of spirits, tongues, and interpretation of tongues. Eight of these gifts are new—the gift of prophecy is repeated from Romans 12.

First Corinthians 12 continues with additional gifts in verse 28. Here eight gifts are alluded to, half of them repeating gifts mentioned earlier: apostles, prophets, teachers, workers of miracles, gifts of healings, helps, governments, diversities of tongues.

Ephesians 4:11 lists five gifts, two of which are new: apostles, prophets, evangelists, pastors, and teachers.

In these three passages, a total of twenty-one different spiritual gifts are mentioned. In additional to these passages, other gifts are suggested in the Bible. First Peter 4:8 indicates that hospitality may well be included as one of the spiritual gifts, and 1 Corinthians 13:3 includes martyrdom as a gift of the Spirit.

Look over these lists to see if any of them catch the attention. Then pray over them and determine whether one or two gifts stand out. This is the purpose of the exploration process—simply to become acquainted with the kind of things the Spirit can gift us with.

During this phase of discovery, one might wish to utilize one of the popular inventories on spiritual gifts. However, a caution is in order here. These spiritual-gifts inventories have been greatly misused. They are meant to help in the exploration process so that a person might pinpoint a good place to begin in discovering his or her gifts. However, the inventory is not meant to convey exactly what a person's gift is. That will not be discovered just by consulting one of the inventories. It will only suggest where to begin. This leads into the third step of the discovery process.

3. Experiment with as many gifts as possible.

As the various listings of spiritual gifts found in the Bible are explored, and as the score on a spiritual-gifts inventory is obtained, it is possible to narrow one's list down to just a few gifts. But a Christian should continue to pray through this stage for God's will in discovering which of these He has given you.

The next step is to begin experimenting with different gifts. In other words, try using them, and see what the results are. Part of giftedness is the ability to do something better and more easily than someone else. That is why people are gifted. Yet people will never know if they have a gift until they try it.

Some gifts are hard to experiment with. You can't jump off a high building to find out if you have the gift of miracles. The gift of martyrdom is also difficult to experiment with. Yet many of the spiritual gifts do lend themselves to experimentation.

One such gift is the gift of evangelism. Most studies have indicated that at least ten percent of a local congregation's active membership has been gifted with this gift, yet fewer than two percent are actually using it. If a person has explored the gifts and discovered that evangelism is near the top of his or her list of possible gifts, how can such a person experiment with it?

First of all, receive training. Just because people are gifted does not mean they do not need training. Suppose a person decides that God has possibly gifted her with the gift of evangelism and that God is leading her to use that gift in giving Bible studies. The first thing she should do is to attend a training program to learn how to give Bible studies. Then she might experiment by accompanying someone who is gifted in that area and observing him or her, before trying to conduct a study. If she finds that this is not her gift, she can easily drop out and try something else.

A caution is in order here. A church in a gift-based ministry must provide freedom for people to experiment with the gifts. A church cannot arbitrarily assign people to an area where they will be locked in for years. If that happens, gift discovery will be seriously hampered. Let people know that they have freedom to move from one area to another as they try out the different gifts.

When we find that we have one gift, we should try another. Remember, God may have gifted us with more than one gift. We are never going to know unless we are willing to keep on experimenting.

4. Examine your feelings.

Feelings are not always the best criteria, but they should certainly be considered when people are discovering their place of ministry or their gifts. As a person experiments with a gift, does he have a sense of satisfaction while doing it? If he has total distaste, it may well be an indication that it is not his gift.

However, don't confuse nervousness or uneasiness the first time something is done with a lack of satisfaction. Many people are very uneasy and nervous the first few times they experiment with employing the gift of evangelism, yet they find afterward that a real sense of satisfaction develops.

God does not ask us to do something we are absolutely miserable doing. That's the whole point of using our gifts. When we use the gifts God has given us, we should and will enjoy it, and our enjoyment will increase the longer we use our gifts. That's why people involved in gift-based ministries have a deep satisfaction with what they are doing. This also contributes to the joy of the Christian, which is another fruit of the Spirit.

5. Evaluate your effectiveness.

Spiritual gifts have a purpose. They are designed to accomplish a specific objective. If that is not happening, a person has reason to question whether she has that gift. For example, in our previous illustration of using the gift of evangelism to give Bible studies, if a person fails to see people come to Christ after she has given several Bible studies, she might rightfully question whether God has called her to that gift and ministry.

Now, we need to be careful here. People tend to under-estimate their own effectiveness. Many Christians, some-times because of low self-esteem, never feel they are accomplishing anything significant for the Lord. So people should not rely solely on their own assessment.

It is a good idea to check with other people to see what they think about our effectiveness. We should ask for several opinions. We must not belittle ourselves, but think posi-tively. Don't boast, but give God the glory for the gifts of the Holy Spirit. Since spiritual gifts operate in the body, one should expect confirmation from the body. We are a part of a total organization—the body of Christ. If we have a spiritual gift, it will fit with others in the church. Other Christians will recognize our gifts and confirm that we have them. If we think we have a gift which others in the church do not agree that we have, we should be very suspicious of our assessment in this regard.

Here again, a climate of affirmation needs to be set up in the church. Members need to be encouraged, when gift-based ministry is in operation, to affirm people in their gifts. When a Christian sees a fellow member doing something well, she should compliment him on his giftedness in that area. As part of the discovery process, it is good to participate with a small group of people who know you. In such a group, participants can take time to share what each person sees to be the spiritual gifts of the others in the group. This can be a wonderfully affirming process for those involved.

These are just five simple steps. However, they really should not be taken independently. Spiritual gifts operate in the body, and a person needs the help of the body in the discovery process. That's why the process described in Chapter 8 is so important. The whole church needs to be involved in the discovery of every member's gifts. That's what it means to be a part of God's church. Let's help each other.

7

Keeping Spiritual
Gifts Alive

M any churches have conducted Spiritual Gifts Seminars or have given some attention at one time or another to spiritual gifts. All too often, however, the emphasis on spiritual gifts has ended with the seminar. No real follow-through has occurred. In this book we are not suggesting that a church simply conduct a Spiritual Gifts Seminar—though that may be a part of the process. We are encouraging churches to make an emphasis on spiritual gifts a way of life. That's why the next chapter will deal exclusively with setting up a gift-based ministry in the local church. The structure of the church will need to change to accommodate the biblical model of spiritual gifts.

Before discussing how to set up a gift-based model of ministry, let us now explore one further question concerning spiritual gifts. Is there some way that we can keep the concept of spiritual gifts constantly before the congregation so that they will never forget it? If a gift-based ministry is foundational for lay involvement, and if lay involvement is such a crucial element in a Christian's life—as the Bible indicates it is—then it certainly is something that needs to be in the forefront of local church life.

The early New Testament church obviously succeeded in keeping spiritual gifts constantly in focus. New believers entered the church, discovered their gifts, and immediately were placed into ministry. That's why the church grew so rapidly. How did these church leaders keep spiritual gifts before their congregations all the time? How did they keep it on the front burner for new converts? How did it happen that as people joined the church, they were eager to discover their gifts?

What I am going to suggest in this chapter is not meant as an obligatory ordinance for all new converts. But I am suggesting that perhaps we could use one of the methods of the early church to keep the reception of spiritual gifts constantly before a congregation. There may be other ways this could be done, but I have found that this biblical example has worked well. It also helps new converts to be enthusiastic about discovering their gift as soon as they join the church.

The Old Testament Priests

The doctrine of the priesthood of all believers is an outgrowth of the Old Testament priesthood. The Old Testament priests entered the priesthood through a special consecration service—a service described in Exodus 29:1-7, where Aaron and his sons are set apart for the priesthood:

> This is what you are to do to consecrate them,
> so they may serve me as priests: Take a young bull
> and two rams without defect. And from fine wheat
> flour, without yeast, make bread, and cakes mixed
> with oil, and wafers spread with oil. Put them in a
> basket and present them in it—along with the bull
> and the two rams. Then bring Aaron and his sons
> to the entrance to the Tent of Meeting and wash
> them with water. Take the garments and dress
> Aaron with the tunic, the robe of the ephod, the

ephod itself and the breastpiece. Fasten the
ephod on him by its skillfully woven waistband.
Put the turban on his head and attach the sacred
diadem to the turban. Take the anointing oil and
anoint him by pouring it on his head, NIV.

When this service was finished, the priest was ordained
and free to begin his ministry.

Four things happened at the ordination of these Old
Testament priests:

■ Aaron and his sons recognized that a sacrifice needed to
be made for their sins. Therefore, the first thing they did
was to offer a sacrifice (vs. 1-3).

■ After offering the sacrifice, Aaron and his sons were
washed in the water of the laver (v. 4). This was the only
time the priest was completely washed in the laver. At
other times, his hands and feet were washed, but at this
time his whole body was washed.

■ Having been washed, the priest was then clothed in new
garments, the vestments of the priestly office (vs. 5, 6).

■ Finally, the head of the priest was anointed with oil,
anointing him for his ministry (v. 7).

The New Testament Priests

In the New Testament, all believers become priests
before God. This is the doctrine of the priesthood of all
believers that we have previously examined. In the New
Testament, however, there is an initiation service into the
priesthood that parallels the ordination service of the priest
in the Old Testament. Notice what happens in the New
Testament when a person comes to Christ:

■ The person must recognize the sacrifice of Jesus Christ
for his sins. Just as the Old Testament priests recognized
that a sacrifice was made for their sins, so the New
Testament believer accepts the sacrifice of Jesus for his

sins as the first step in coming to Christ and preparing to become His minister.

■ Having accepted the sacrifice of Christ, the believer is baptized. Just as the Old Testament priest was washed in the laver, the New Testament believer is washed in the rite of Bible baptism.

■ Coming out of the water, the individual is clothed in the garments of Christ's righteousness—the garments of the New Testament priesthood. Again, there is a parallel with the Old Testament service. Here, however, the parallel ends for most churches. At baptism the emphasis is on cleansing from sin—and rightly so. There is rejoicing that the individual has been redeemed.

But redeemed for what? There seems to be something missing in our baptismal ceremony—something that should draw attention to the fact that the call of Christ is not just to receive cleansing but to enter ministry for Him.

The Old Testament consecration service concluded with the anointing of the priest. This signified recognition on the part of God and the church that the individual had been called to ministry. Only after the anointing was the priest to perform ministry. Could it be that the failure of most churches to provide a parallel service to the Old Testament anointing may be the reason that very few converts are immediately placed into ministry?

The example of Jesus in the New Testament conveys the idea that baptism is even more of a believer's ordination to ministry than it is a cleansing from sin. Jesus was not baptized to be cleansed from sin. He was baptized as our example, to be sure, but even more to authenticate the fact that He was about to enter His ministry. After His baptism, the Holy Spirit descended in the form of a dove and anointed Jesus for His ministry. On this momentous occasion, Jesus was given a visible sign that baptism inaugurated His ministry through the Holy Spirit.

As we study the early church, we quickly discover that its leaders had a way of letting people know they were called to ministry. It seems logical that we should follow this New Testament practice so that new converts, as well as older members, see the Christian life as an ordination to ministry.

How the Early Church Recognized Calls to Ministry

While the Holy Spirit visibly fell on Christ at His baptism, this did not happen with subsequent baptisms in the New Testament. Instead, the early church had a way of showing that the invisible Holy Spirit was being poured out on people to anoint them for their ministry. A study of the New Testament reveals that they utilized a simple means to publicly recognize an individual's call to ministry. Many times this recognition was of clergy ministry; other times, of deacons and elders; and sometimes they even recognized a new convert's call to ministry. In each of these instances, this recognition was demonstrated through the laying on of hands.

> While they were worshiping the Lord and fasting, the Holy Spirit said, "Set apart for me Barnabas and Saul for the work to which I have called them." So after they had fasted and prayed, they placed their hands on them and sent them off. —Acts 13:2, 3, NIV.

While this is a case of clergy being set apart and anointed for ministry, it does show that the method used to recognize a call to ministry was the laying on of hands.

> Do not neglect your gift, which was given you through a prophetic message when the body of elders laid their hands on you. —1 Timothy 4:14, NIV.

And while this text could possibly be referring to young Timothy's ordination to the function of clergy, it could also refer to a laying on of hands that might have coincided with his conversion. The interesting point here is that Paul indicates that Timothy received a spiritual gift in connection with the laying on of hands. Could it be that laying on of hands is an indication that the Holy Spirit has fallen on an individual and given that person spiritual gifts?

Since spiritual gifts are in no way the exclusive domain of the clergy, we must be careful that we don't refer this text exclusively to clergy, or it would be easy to conclude that pastors receive spiritual gifts at the laying on of hands at their ordination to the gospel ministry. While they may receive additional gifts for use with their pastoral role, they should already have received some gifts of the Spirit when they were converted.

Actually, the New Testament seems to imply that the doctrine of the laying on of hands is not to be reserved solely for elders, deacons, and clergy. Note how the author of Hebrews sets forth the laying on of hands as one of the elementary doctrines of the Christian faith.

> Therefore let us leave the elementary
> teachings about Christ and go on to maturity, not
> laying again the foundation of repentance from
> acts that lead to death, and of faith in God,
> instruction about baptisms, the laying on of hands,
> the resurrection of the dead, and eternal
> judgment.—Hebrews 6:1, 2, NIV.

According to Hebrews, the doctrine of the laying on of hands is one of the elementary doctrines of the Christian faith, along with repentance and faith. How could that be, if laying on of hands is reserved only for clergy, elders, or deacons? In these ordinations, much is required—and the church is admonished not to lay hands on them too quickly. Yet there seems to be a New Testament doctrine that places the laying on of hands in the elementary stages of the Christian life.

Did the early church practice laying on of hands at the time of conversion? Do we have any New Testament examples of the laying on of hands being used in this elementary sense—with new converts? There are at least two examples:

> When the apostles in Jerusalem heard that Samaria had accepted the word of God, they sent Peter and John to them. When they arrived, they prayed for them that they might receive the Holy Spirit, because the Holy Spirit had not yet come upon any of them; they had simply been baptized into the name of the Lord Jesus. Then Peter and John placed their hands on them, and they received the Holy Spirit.—Acts 8:14-17, NIV.

Here were brand-new converts, just coming to Christ. The disciples heard that they had received the Lord and sent Peter and John to them. They had been baptized, but now as a sign that they also had received the Holy Spirit, Peter and John laid their hands on them, effectively ordaining them to the ministry of the regular church member. Remember, the Holy Spirit is poured out in connection with the reception of spiritual gifts that enable members to minister. This seems to be what Peter and John were practicing. The way they publicly recognized it was through the laying on of hands.

Not only did Peter and John practice the laying on of hands for new converts, but the apostle Paul also demonstrated the acceptability of this custom:

> While Apollos was at Corinth, Paul took the road through the interior and arrived at Ephesus. There he found some disciples and asked them, "Did you receive the Holy Spirit when you believed?" They answered, "No, we have not even heard that there is a Holy Spirit." So Paul asked, "Then what baptism did you receive?" "John's baptism," they replied. Paul said, "John's baptism was a baptism of repentance. He told the people to believe in the one coming after him, that is, in Jesus." On hearing this, they were baptized into

the name of the Lord Jesus. When Paul placed his
hands on them, the Holy Spirit came on them,
and they spoke in tongues and prophesied.—Acts
19:1-6, NIV.

Here again were new converts who had been baptized
but had not yet participated in the ministry of the Holy
Spirit, which entailed receiving spiritual gifts and being
involved in ministry. Notice that Paul felt that these people
who had recently been baptized but not placed into ministry
were not yet fully Christians; therefore he rebaptized them
and then laid hands on them, ordaining them to the ministry
of the church member. Ellen White, in commenting on this
passage, says:

> They were baptized in the name of Jesus, and
> as Paul laid his hands upon them, they received
> also the baptism of the Holy Spirit, by which they
> were enabled to speak the languages of other
> nations, and to prophesy. Thus they were qualified
> to serve as missionaries in Ephesus and its vicinity,
> and also to go forth to proclaim the gospel in Asia
> Minor.—*Acts of the Apostles,* p. 283.

Evidently the early church used the laying on of hands
to keep constantly before the believers the need for all
converts to Christianity to find a gift-based ministry in
harmony with the Holy Spirit. They felt so strongly about it
that seemingly, at times, they rebaptized people who were
not involved in ministry. This certainly is in sharp contrast
to today's Christianity, which allows people to be considered
members in good and regular standing even though not
involved in ministry.

Perhaps it would be a good idea for the contemporary
church to follow the New Testament example of the laying
on of hands for new church members. This would accomplish two things.

First, it would keep the idea of spiritual gifts and every-member involvement in ministry constantly before the congregation. Every time a baptism occurred, the need for gift-based ministry would be held up before the congregation.

Second, it would make it necessary for pastors to teach spiritual gifts and the need for ministry involvement to all new converts. They would need to explain to them that baptism is entrance into ministry as well as cleansing from sin.

In churches where this has been tried, new converts enter the church with excitement about finding their place of ministry in the local congregation. As a result, they are enthusiastic about joining a spiritual gifts class. They enter the church with the expectation that they must get involved in ministry.

How should such an ordination service be conducted? It should not be an emotional service. It was not so in the early church. It was simply a recognition that every member has been called to ministry. To recognize that call, the church lays hands on them, signifying that the Christian life is ministry.

After the baptism, candidates can be called forward as usual to receive the hand of fellowship. A few words of explanation can be given, explaining that the priesthood of all believers demands that all Christians be involved in ministry. Baptism signifies one's entrance into the Christian life of ministry. In recognition of that calling, it can be pointed out, we follow the New Testament practice of laying on of hands, which is the recognition by the church that these new converts have been called into ministry and that God has bestowed spiritual gifts upon them for their ministry. Then the pastor can charge the new converts publicly to discover their gifts and to find their place of ministry in harmony with their gifts.

The elders and pastor can then kneel in prayer and at the proper time, lay hands on the new believers, commissioning them for their ministry. Another variation would be to ask the persons who brought them into the church to stand with them and lay hands on them as the pastor prays.

There may be other ways to keep this concept of "every member a minister" before the congregation. This is one way that has strong New Testament backing. Most church members have commented, when they have seen it done, that they have often wondered why the church did not practice this custom of the early church. Perhaps, as part of a new orientation to a gift-based ministry, it is time to give public recognition to the call of the church member to that ministry.

8

Time for a
New Beginning

As you have been reading these pages, perhaps it has already dawned on you that the local church must be restructured if it is to return to God's ideal for effective ministry. If the laity are to be the performers of ministry and the pastors their trainers, the church will definitely need restructuring.

Our churches currently do not facilitate the discovery of gifts and the placing of people into gift-based ministries. Instead, our current system seems to foster putting people into "jobs" rather than "ministries." And these jobs tend to fulfill the needs of the institution rather than those of the individual. So a decision by the local church to initiate a gift-based ministry program will mean that serious changes need to take place.

It's time for a new beginning!

What Is Lay Ministry?

Lay ministry is not just getting church members to do

jobs the clergy feel they should do. Instead, lay ministry is enabling members to accomplish the mission of the church, and at the same time to find personal fulfillment through the ministry in which they are involved.

Both of these purposes must be fulfilled. Lay ministry does not accomplish the task of the church at the expense of its members. Lay ministry does not "use" people; it keeps a proper balance between the mission of the church and the development of people.

Since lay ministry involves not just the task of the church but the development of people, the church must provide multiple options for ministry. People differ, and their individual needs also differ. If they are to find fulfillment in ministry, they must be offered multiple options for ministry. The church must also be adaptable to people creating new kinds of ministries in which to utilize their gifts.

The longer a local church exists, the more likely it is to make the survival and perpetuation of the church its primary goal, until eventually the members become slaves to perpetuating the institution. A people-oriented lay ministry program will change regularly, because people in our current society move and change at an ever-increasing pace. Therefore, if the lay ministry program is people centered rather than institution centered, the church should be constantly updating its training and ministry opportunities to keep abreast of the changing needs of its people. The purpose of these ministries will not change, but the means of achieving them will.

When the church speaks of lay ministry, most members envision involvement in some kind of outreach or nurture ministry sponsored by the established structure of the local church. However, this view must change in order for true lay ministry to take place. Lay ministry occurs not just in the church, but also—and more often—in the world. The members must begin to see that their ministry for Christ might occur on Monday morning at the office rather than on Sabbath morning at church.

The church must realize that lay ministry involves the entire life of the Christian. Ministry is not confined to the church building or to the sacred hours of the Sabbath. The most meaningful ministry for church members may happen in a secular environment during the week. In this view of lay ministry, the church member no longer needs to feel that being involved in ministry means to take a job offered by the church to perpetuate its institutional needs.

It is time for Adventist Christians to break out of their cocoon, to move out of the fortress and integrate into the community, that the world may see the dynamic difference Christ can make in one's life.

Gearing Up the Church for Lay Ministry

It should be apparent by now that the lay ministry we are considering demands that the church reexamine the structure currently in place for involving people in ministry. It may need a drastic overhaul.

Most Adventist churches operate on the basis that the nominating committee must select people in order for them to serve in a "job" or even in a "ministry" within the church. Actually, nominating committees may be more of a hindrance to lay ministry than a help. We may actually be structuring our church in such a way that people are kept out of ministry rather than placed into ministry.

Most nominating committees play a cat-and-mouse game with members. They meet to guess what people would like to do; then the committee twists members' arms to try to get them to accept a job. As a result, many times people are given jobs for which they are not gifted. This results in poor performance, frustration, and sometimes resignation from all church jobs. Nominating committees then endlessly meet, trying to fill positions in the church.

As a first step in restructuring for lay ministry, begin at least to negotiate how nominating committees function. Usually the process begins with a list of jobs which the committee tries to fill. In the lay-ministry approach to the nominating committee, the process begins instead with the membership list. It considers each person—his or her gifts and desires (which have been submitted to the committee)—as well as the needs of the church. The nominating committee then proceeds through the membership list, placing people into positions that harmonize with their personal needs and spiritual gifts.

In churches where the author has tried this approach, it has revolutionized the nominating committee process. Instead of spending endless meetings attempting to fill positions, the committee rarely has had to meet again after completing their review of the membership list. Since the positions are in harmony with members' gifts and desires, the members gladly accept them—no drawn-out persuasion is necessary, and no members reluctantly accept positions out of a misguided sense of duty.

While this is a good first step, it should be viewed as just that. It is not the final solution. Eventually, the church may wish to abolish the nominating committee entirely and substitute in its place an ongoing committee, which might be called the Lay Ministry Committee. Its task would be to place people in ministry in harmony with their spiritual gifts. This would be done not once a year, but continuously as new people join or as people feel the need for new assignments.

Another problem with nominating committees is that they attempt to fill too many positions. One church of six hundred in attendance was actually attempting to fill five hundred positions. That herculean task would destroy any church and its nominating committee, especially if repeated every year. Yet this is the problem, as most churches are currently structured. People need approval or a specific invitation from the nominating committee for whatever they do in the church. Sometimes we even add or "create" positions so that people will feel needed. This then becomes one more job to fill in the future. In the long run, the endless list of jobs that we create discourages people and hinders lay involvement.

Sometimes we create so many jobs that little time is left for the average church member to get involved in meaningful ministry. Many of the most gifted people in the church use all their available "church" time sitting on boards and committees. Certainly there is a better use for their time than that. Any church that is serious about lay ministry will need to streamline the church structure to allow people to have time to be involved in ministry. Some might disagree, but I would like to suggest that sitting on committees is not ministry—certainly not in the active sense necessary for the church to finish its mission on earth.

One of the complaints heard most often by church officers is that they do not have time to be involved in the "mission" activities of the church. Pastors sometimes respond to that by laying guilt trips on these people. However, it is time the church took that complaint seriously. The church needs to recognize that in today's stress-filled society, people realistically have only a certain amount of time that they can devote to the church.

For some, that may be five hours a week—outside of attending Sabbath School and church. It is possible that the church might be able to convince a few people to increase their ministry time to six or seven hours, but rarely beyond that. This does not mean, necessarily, that people who commit less time are not as dedicated. The church needs to recognize that people's secular jobs and businesses occupy enormous amounts of time today.

Here, for example, is Brother John. John is a local elder and a Sabbath School teacher. In order to do his job well in the church, John will need to spend a minimum of three hours a week just preparing the Sabbath School lesson. In addition, because he is an elder, he will probably be assigned to sit on various church committees, such as the church board, the personal ministries committee, the Sabbath School council, the finance committee, or the stewardship committee. He could well spend two or three nights per week just sitting on church committees. In addition, as an elder, he is expected to spend one night each week visiting church members. Yet he rarely visits because of all the committees.

Brother John then hears the pleas to be involved in mission activities that reach people for Christ, but he has no time. He is already committed to six or seven hours for the church each week. Any more, and his family would really complain. The church sometimes has made these people feel guilty for not being more involved and has caused them actually to neglect their families. That is a crime! With the breakup of Adventist homes occurring at alarming rates, the church must make certain it does not overwork people and keep them from their families. We must not destroy families in the name of Christ.

Obviously, Brother John is at the capacity of his church involvement with the present structure. Yet he feels frustrated because he sees so little accomplished from all his committee work. He wishes he could do more, but all of his time is occupied in maintaining the institution of the church. What can be done? Obviously, Brother John cannot be asked to do more, but perhaps it is possible to streamline the church structure, so that he doesn't have to sit on so many committees. Then he would be free for lay ministry.

What is happening to Brother John is happening to too many church members. They are so busy just running and maintaining the church that they have no time to be involved in ministry. Since members follow their leaders, and the leaders spend no time in mission, it is only natural that very few members show any interest in mission-oriented lay ministry. Perhaps we need to eliminate some of the positions in the church in order to free people for ministry.

Someone might ask, "What positions can we eliminate?" Every position is considered important by someone, it seems. Pastor Ron Gladden, when pastor of the Madison, Wisconsin, SDA Church, attempted to institute a people-centered ministry approach instead of the "job" approach so common in most churches. As part of that process, he discussed with his church what positions were absolutely necessary in order for it to be a Seventh-day Adventist church. What happened?

> We looked at the list, discussed each slot
> individually (sometimes with vigor!), then crossed
> most of them off. When the dust settled, we had
> retained four: head elder, head deacon, treasurer,
> and clerk. (Head deaconess would normally be
> included, but our churches use "deacon" to refer
> to both men and women.)[1]

Amazing! And we thought we needed all these jobs! So much of what we do as a church is busy work. It is not helping us accomplish our mission, but may actually be preventing that from happening.

Pastor Gladden, having freed his people from the burden of the institutional needs of the church, organized the church around involvement in various ministries. This is what is meant by the phrase "lay ministry church."

Care should be taken not to just rename positions as ministries and then proceed as usual. Remember, ministries are developed around the needs of the members and focused on accomplishing the mission of the church. This does not mean the church will not have a Sabbath School, but it may mean that the Sabbath School will be much different. It also means that those involved will have greater satisfaction.

Basic Requirements for a Lay Ministry Program

For an effective lay ministry program to operate on the local level, five basic requirements are necessary.

■ There must be a long-term commitment to the concept and its implications. A church may not begin a lay ministry program one year, only to revert to the previous model the next year. The restructuring necessary and the time needed to fully develop the program means that a church will need to commit to this new approach for the long haul. A minimum of three to five years is essential to adequately develop a lay ministry program. However, as a church sees its membership coming to life, it should fairly quickly witness some positive results from this experiment of allowing the laity to really be the church. Our commitment to lay ministry must not occur simply to implement another program of the church; it must be seen instead as a serious attempt to return to the New Testament model of laity.

■ Second, lay ministry demands church-wide support. The commitment of only a few members will not be sufficient. Any church that wishes to experiment in this direction will need to plan the process carefully, so that as many people as possible understand what is happening and are committed to its accomplishment. Discussions in small church committees, a definite commitment from the church board, sermons from the pulpit, and perhaps widespread distribution of this book among the membership will help a church see the necessity of this approach to ministry.

■ Third, a commitment to lay ministry will require leadership. A pastor who is not an ardent supporter of this concept will not be able to lead his church into a lay ministry structure. This concept can in fact be very threatening to pastors who have been trained to be the "minister." They may be reluctant to release the laity for ministry. Pastors also must not push the laity too fast, because laity have been accustomed to the pastor being the minister, and it may be difficult for them to change their thinking. Therefore, strong leadership that gently leads the church is needed in the implementation of this concept.

■ Fourth, implementation of a lay ministry program will require a good information-management system. If a church has a computer, a good database software package that can store and retrieve all the pertinent information about each of the members should be used. Not only will the church need a way to retrieve the information once stored, but it will also need to develop a survey instrument to obtain the information from the membership in the first place. Information to be gathered in such a survey might include: members' spiritual gifts, jobs previously held in the church, current ministry involvement, hopes and desires for further involvement, time available, and so on.

■ Finally, the church will need to have a regular system of providing training for the people who are involved in these on-going ministries. Ministry involvement will necessitate a strong training program in the church. We will discuss this further in a later chapter.

Steps in Restructuring

Before concluding this chapter, let's summarize the steps that will be needed as we restructure the church for lay ministry:

1. The church will need a clear understanding of lay ministry. Lay ministry is fulfilling the mission of the church through people who grow spiritually by their involvement.

2. Lay ministry is people centered rather than institution centered. Therefore, the purpose of ministry is the enhancement of people rather than just caring for institutional needs.

3. A first step in restructuring the church for lay ministry is to have the nominating committee fill current positions based on the needs of the members rather than on the needs of the church. Any positions not filled are eliminated. If God wants the position filled, He will gift someone for the position.

4. A more radical approach would be to eliminate most jobs

currently performed in the church. The four or five that are left can be appointed by the nominating committee. The rest of the church is then organized around ministries. People are then placed into these ministries through the Lay Ministry Committee, whose main job is to get people involved in harmony with their giftedness. As long as a person is satisfied and is doing a good job, that person remains in the ministry. When the person wishes to be involved differently, the Lay Ministry Committee works with the individual on a new assignment in harmony with the present gifts of the member.

5. These ministries may occur as the person ministers for Christ in the church—or in the world. The whole point of a lay ministry structure in the local church is to free God's people to minister for Christ in the world and not to be confined to the church. It is time for the church to remove its walls and become the salt of the earth, as Jesus wants it to be.

Obviously, this is a radical departure from the way most churches currently operate. Much prayer, study, and discussion needs to go into the process of transforming an existing church into a lay ministry model. The next two chapters will center on involving people in ministry in harmony with their spiritual gifts and establishing a base for ministry training in the local church.

It's time for a new beginning for the Adventist Church as it seeks to finish the work of God by restructuring itself to make ministry a way of life for all its members.

Notes:

1. Ron Gladden, *The Drama of Church Recruiting* (unpublished manuscript).

9

How to Place Members Into Ministry

In the previous chapter, we outlined the possibilities of setting up a gift-based ministry in the local church instead of one that is job-based. To accomplish this, the mental attitude of the church must be one of commitment to a gift-based ministry. This chapter, then, is essential for those churches which wish to pursue a gift-based ministry.

Placing people into ministry, however, is one of the most difficult parts of the process. Many churches have seen the need for a gift-based ministry and have realized that the laity must be empowered for ministry, but they have not known how to accomplish it.

Churches may conduct Spiritual Gifts Seminars, preach sermons on spiritual gifts, and rally the troops for involvement, but unless they actually go on to deploy people into active, gift-based ministry, nothing of lasting impact will emerge.

A church must meet several prerequisites before it is ready to dispatch its members into ministry. Let's consider them.

■ First, there must be a high level of commitment on the part of the local church to a lay ministry structure based on spiritual gifts. This commitment will have been attained through seminars, sermons, and group discussions, especially among the leadership.

■ Second, a church that is ready to deploy people into ministry will have begun the people-centered approach to ministry discussed in the previous chapter. In other words, ministry involvement is people-centered rather than institution-centered. The emphasis is on helping people find fulfillment in ministry rather than on filling the needs of the institution.

■ Third, the church will have conducted at least one Spiritual Gifts Seminar. During the seminar, people may have used one of the spiritual gifts inventories, but more importantly, they will have discussed spiritual gifts in group settings and begun the discovery process. The seminar does not need to be long or involved. In fact, the simpler the church can keep it, the more effective it will be.

These are the prerequisites to becoming involved in the deployment stage of a gift-based ministry. Many churches have seen no results following their Spiritual Gift Seminars because they have seen the seminar as the final step rather than the prerequisite to involvement. If the church does nothing more than conduct the seminar, nothing much will happen. The steps discussed below are crucial in the process.

The Ministry Placement Interview

Following the Spiritual Gifts Seminar, a ministry placement interview should be conducted with each seminar participant. This interview will probably be conducted by the pastor as a church begins the transition to a gift-based ministry. However, the pastor should be training someone else to do this. Therefore, it is imperative that the interview be conducted by the pastor with a trainee observing. Eventually, as the church continues to progress in gift-based ministries, a special lay ministry committee could be set up, the main task of which would be to conduct this ministry placement interview and follow it up to make certain each person becomes involved in ministry.

The work of this committee—or of the pastor—will be very heavy at the beginning of the process as the existing membership is being placed into ministry. However, after the initial thrust, the committee's responsibility will shift to the newcomers to the church. In order to help ease into the process, it might be well to limit the size of the first Spiritual Gifts Seminar to the number the church feels it can adequately follow up and place in ministry.

The purpose of the ministry placement interview is to review with each member the results of the Spiritual Gifts Seminar—and particularly the results of the spiritual gifts inventory—as well as observations that other members have made during the seminar regarding the member's spiritual gifts. Other areas that should be explored during the interview would be the member's present satisfaction with church involvement and any other areas of ministry in which he or she might be interested.

It is important, as a part of this process, to thoroughly discuss with members where they envision their involvement. At this stage of the visit, it is important to carefully listen. Hopefully, out of this listening process, an area of interest will begin to emerge.

The second purpose of the interview is to set specific

steps that the member and the church should take in the coming months to find a ministry appropriate to his spiritual gifts, strengths, interests, and concerns. This series of steps should be written out and given to the individual, with a copy kept by the church.

Guidelines for the Interview

In order for the church successfully to conduct the ministry placement interview, the following guidelines are suggested:

1. The interview should be conducted either in the member's home or in the church office—never over the telephone. If ministry placement is as important as we have indicated in this book, then it deserves a face-to-face visit.

2. The person conducting the interview should remember that the purpose of lay ministry is not to place the member in a church job, but rather to enable the member to find personal fulfillment in the ministry that is selected. At the same time, however, the interviewer should not forget that the mission of the church is to make disciples, and that making disciples involves both outreach and nurture ministries.

The interviewer should try to bring together the needs of the individual and the mission of the church and resist the temptation to "use" the member for the purpose of placing her where there is a need in the organization, rather than a need in the individual. At the same time, the interviewer should make certain that the ministry will contribute to the overall mission of the church.

3. The interviewer should refrain from being either judgmental or forceful. The purpose of the interview is for the interviewer and the member to come to some sense of direction using the specific steps needed to discover a ministry. The interviewer should not convey the impression that he knows all the answers. Gift discovery is an effort that

involves the entire body, and the member should certainly be involved in determining her own destiny. If she feels she has been "delegated" or pressured into a ministry or job, she will not have nearly the sense of ownership she will, when she is the one who determines her own ministry-discovery steps. The interviewer should be sensitive, caring, and empathetic, do a lot of listening, and keep the member's concerns and priorities foremost in mind.

4. The interviewer should ascertain what the individual member's particular expectations are about her place in the church, and what her image of an "ideal" ministry would involve. Then they should work together in identifying specific steps to realize that joy of service. At the same time, they should keep in mind that the goal of ministry is giving and serving, not receiving. The question is, Where can the member serve most effectively and joyfully?

5. Time should be taken during the interview to discuss the member's apprehensions, if she has any, about ministry. What are her misgivings, hesitations, concerns, or fears? Don't be afraid to bring these out into the open. Otherwise they will fester and prevent fulfillment in the ministry she has chosen.

6. The interviewer should resist the temptation to discuss only present ministry opportunities in the church. God may have placed it on the hearts of some of these members to begin an entirely new ministry. Don't stifle the Spirit by limiting ministries to those currently existing. Often the most effective and fulfilling ministries of a church are in the future, and they may be different from what the church is currently doing.

This does not mean that every member should start a new ministry. Those who are gifted to start a new ministry are few and far between. Neither must new ministries be ruled out of the picture by the church. There may be people in the church whom God has gifted in an area that could significantly broaden the church's ministry and enhance the member's individual ministry in the same process.

7. The interviewer should discuss with the member the possible need of training for performing effective ministry. The fact that individuals are gifted does not mean that they do not need training. Perhaps they could perform the ministry without training, but their ministry would be significantly enhanced if proper training were given. If the members have no previous experience, then training is indispensable.

8. The interviewer should remember that the primary purpose of this interview is to identify some specific steps to be taken by the member in the next several months to find her ministry. Specific dates should be set for completion of each step. Near the end of the interview, the goal is to agree on the appropriate steps to be taken.

These steps may vary from having the person give further study to the discovery of her gift, to enrolling in a Bible study training program, visiting a Pathfinder meeting for the next month, or any other specific step. Every ministry placement interview should result in a completed set of steps, dates, and responsibilities laid out in writing.

9. As the visit proceeds, definite ministries or roles will surface in which the member may wish to be involved. If there is to be involvement in an existing ministry, the first step would be to allow the member to observe the ministry or role for at least a month without commitment. That will help the member decide in a noncommittal context if this ministry is for her. It also gives her a chance to evaluate her feelings about the role, as well as to receive feedback from others about her effectiveness and ability to work with others as she fulfills the expectations of the position. Thus, after the experimental period, it is imperative that a member of the Lay Ministry Committee interview the member again to review and analyze what has happened.

After the Interview

After the interview is completed and a set of expectations is drawn up, the person conducting the interview should give the member a copy of the steps to be followed and file a copy with the church office. The interviewer would then need to follow up the visit by making certain that the steps are implemented. For example, if the person decided that God had gifted her for children's ministry, and she saw that the best place to use her gift in the church was in the Junior Department, then one of the first steps would be for the interviewer to contact the Junior Department leader and arrange for the member to spend a noncommittal month in that department. The Junior Department leader would then contact the member and arrange for her to get involved.

The above-mentioned step is crucial to ministry involvement. The responsibility of making these connections should never rest upon the member; otherwise, nothing much will happen. Any contacts that might need to be made, based upon the steps drawn up with the member, should be made within one week of the interview. If the member does not begin involvement soon after the interview, it may be more difficult later.

If the person wishes to begin a new ministry, which will require church funding, one of the steps will be to have the person present his new ministry idea to the church board or Church Ministries Council for approval. The person representing the Lay Ministry Committee should help facilitate this presentation to the board.

Following the procedures outlined in this chapter is probably one of the most crucial steps in the involvement process. Failure to do this is one of the main reasons lay people get motivated and trained but not deployed into ministry.

This process will require much time and effort, but ministry involvement will prove to be worth the investment. As the church begins its transition, the pastor may conduct most of these interviews. The wise pastor, however, will involve other members in the process, training them also to conduct the interview. Eventually this procedure will require less pastoral attention. Remember that the primary focus of the church that operates on this model is to involve the members in some kind of meaningful ministry.

Some may feel that their church cannot accomplish lay ministry because of all the internal problems they are facing. Yet lay ministry may be the best way to solve some of those problems. As someone has said: "The best remedy for a sick church is to put it to work." This does not mean that we can ignore all problems, but many of our petty difficulties will vanish when the church is fully employed.

The accomplishment of member ministry involvement means a change in the attitudes of both clergy and laity, as well as a restructuring of the church to a ministry base instead of a job base. However, it can be done. It must be done. And it will be done by the grace of God.

Let's begin the process.

10

Training for Ministry

The primary task of the pastor, according to Scripture, is to train or equip the members for their ministry. Much of the pastor's time should be spent in helping members discover a place of ministry in harmony with their spiritual gifts. We have discussed this process in the preceding chapter. However, merely placing people into ministries does not insure that they will be competent, even if they are gifted. Training is an absolutely vital component that will require significant pastoral attention if people are to function effectively in ministry.

Good training is reinforced by good ministry descriptions. Too often people have accepted a role or task in the church without fully understanding the expectations and requirements. Before people are deployed into ministry, they should be supplied with a clearly written job description for that ministry and an explanation of the involvement that is expected from them.

This job description should include not only the tasks required in the ministry, but also some of the skills and spiritual gifts needed to adequately perform the functions of the ministry. In addition, it should include such things as the name of the person to whom the member is responsible, whom they should contact for support, and what training the church would recommend to fit the person for involvement in that ministry.

If all of these factors are carefully formulated before the member accepts the assignment, many misunderstandings will be avoided, and the member will feel far more comfortable serving his Lord. The area of training is one that must be given adequate attention to enable church members to get involved in meaningful ministry.

As one person has suggested, the local church is really a "mini-seminary, of which the pastor is the dean." Since one of the primary responsibilities of the church is to serve as a training center for Christian workers, the training needs should have priority in budgeting, as well as in allocation of time.

Most local church training occurring today is not systematic or intentional; rather, it occurs because someone feels a burden to provide training in a certain area. There is no centralized effort to equip all the members for their ministries. The Adventist church has developed superb resources for training in many areas of church life. Sadly, these are very seldom used in most churches. Under financial squeezes, most churches opt not to purchase the needed resources or feel that these resources ought to be provided at no charge. However, when resources are made available at no charge, few churches use them, because they have no vested interest in them.

If training is to be one of the priority functions of the Adventist church, then it is necessary that money be allocated from the local church budget for training materials and that quality time be given to training in the church calendar.

Some conferences, recognizing the limited resources in many small local churches, have opted for a conference-wide program of training, in which people from various churches come to a central location for a weekend or a Sabbath to receive specialized training. This is essential and must continue, but if the church truly is to be a training center, then more training than this must be made available. Conference-wide events must be seen as a supplement to the local church training program, not as a substitution for it.

Few members from a single local church will attend the conference-wide training event. Many times even the pastor is not present and does not know what is being presented. Those who attend return from the training event fired up, enthused, and ready for action. The members who were not involved, however, do not feel the same conviction. The members who attended are sometimes resisted or ignored—and little happens. Sometimes they even become discouraged.

A local church training center may be small, but some training ought to be taking place on a regular basis in every local Seventh-day Adventist church. Some very small churches may wish to combine with other churches in the district to provide a district-wide training program.

In introducing a Lay Ministry Training Center at the local church level, bear in mind that we are not discussing occasional training programs, but a regular, systematic, and intentional course offering that will effectively train the members of the church.

Some of this training will be general. People involved in many different kinds of ministries could avail themselves of such training. Other training will be very specific, providing instruction for a special ministry in the local church. When a member enters a ministry in a church that functions with a Lay Ministry Training Center, he is given a list of courses he should take to be equipped for that particular ministry. The church then is responsible to ensure that those courses are offered over a reasonable period of time in that church. Some courses may be offered several times. Larger churches may offer many courses at once, while smaller churches would probably offer only one course at a time.

Providing adequate training for all church members involved in ministry means that there is consistency in various ministries when personnel change, because the training has been similar for each person involved in those ministries. Because regular training is provided, people have the opportunity to fully develop their spiritual gifts. This will enable them to move into different ministries that require using some of their less-developed gifts. Because people are continually changing, new ministries and new places for working will be continually developing. Thus training will need to be ongoing.

Providing good training sends a message to all church members that their ministry is important. Otherwise, why would the church be willing to provide such good training for them? Therefore, the expertise and skills of the members continually increase as they perform in the various ministries.

Training should especially be provided in the areas of the church that enhance its vision and mission. As a result, members will quickly discover what the church considers important. More members will not only catch the vision of the church, but will actively contribute to that which the church feels is vital.

When we think of training, we naturally reflect on the training of church members, but perhaps we need also to look at training as a vehicle to create bridges with the community served by our church. Many of the courses taught in the local Lay Ministry Training Center may be of interest to people in the community. For example, a church may conduct a Marriage Enrichment Seminar as part of its lay training emphasis on the home. Community people will benefit just as much as church members from such a course.

In addition to conducting courses that can train members and non-members, the local church's Lay Ministry Training Center could sponsor classes developed especially for the people in the community. For example, in one church I pastored, we conducted three or four classes each week on a specific night of the week. One of those classes was specifically geared so that members could bring their friends. One time we offered a class in auto mechanics, taught by a member who was an instructor in auto mechanics in the local school system. Other times we offered classes in ceramics or similar non-threatening types of classes. Many non-members attended.

Many of these community people, who may have initially attended a first aid class, developed the habit of regularly attending these classes. Knowing that other classes were taught on the same evening, they later enrolled in other classes—such as a cooking school or a Revelation Seminar. In that sense, it was possible to make even the training event evangelistic.

Since most of the topics geared for the non-member were non-biblical, our primary task was for members and non-members to build relationships. Friendships are the major reason people choose churches in the first place. A church that builds a training program that will help people enhance their relationships with non-members is working wisely.

How to Organize a Lay Ministry Training Center

Once a church has decided to operate a local Lay Ministry Training Center, planning for the operation of such a program should quickly begin. One of the first areas to consider is curriculum. What courses will the church teach—and when? Will the church teach several courses on a particular evening once a week—or will it offer only one course at a time?

Some of the kinds of classes a church might consider teaching are courses in lay ministries skills—ushering; teaching a Sabbath School class; training as an elder, deacon, or deaconess. The choir could even practice on this particular night as a separate group. Any role that a lay person assumes in the local church should require some kind of minimal training. That could be provided here.

In addition, there are several general areas of training that many church members could avail themselves of—classes in biblical studies to enhance a member's understanding of certain Bible books, such as Romans, Galatians, Daniel and Revelation, or a general Bible survey.

Other classes might focus on the family, communication, expectations of new church members, discovering spiritual gifts, and so on.

Specific courses on witnessing and evangelism should be a vital part of the curriculum. In this section would be classes on friendship evangelism, witnessing, giving Bible studies, gaining decisions, conducting seminars, and similar topics.

The fourth area of the curriculum would be the area of community interest. In this section the church would periodically provide classes especially geared to the community. This is where the class in auto mechanics would fit, as well as classes in first aid, drugs, taxes, and so on. In addition, the church should provide classes on specific biblical subjects to help community people come to Christ and the church. Thus, at least once a year, one of the classes should be a Revelation/Prophecy Seminar or similar program. As people become interested, they could be invited to small groups in the church, where they could also begin to interact spiritually with other church members.

The biggest barrier most churches face in starting a lay ministry training program is finding qualified teachers. That's why a small church must start small, perhaps offering only one class at a time. However, the church need not limit its selection of teachers to church members alone. Perhaps the friend of a member would be willing to teach a class on auto repair. This person's involvement may even be a means of introducing him to Christ.

Conference personnel who are gifted in a certain area could be invited to conduct a class periodically. Even a video class could be taught, utilizing many of the excellent video courses currently available from the North American Division. If the church is really committed to this process, it will find an adequate supply of teachers for the classes it needs. If a certain kind of teacher is required, and none is available in the local congregation, perhaps the church should postpone the class until God sends the right teacher. In the meantime, the members should earnestly pray that God will send them the right person to teach the class. The church will be amazed at how eager God is to answer those prayers.

Some churches have carried the training concept one step further by credentialing as lay ministers those who have completed certain levels of training. This does not mean that those individuals have no more need of training, but that they have completed the required classes and have demonstrated ability in their ministry. Once every six months or once a year, the church publicly recognizes, through some kind of credentialing service, those who have completed the training. This public recognition encourages others to get involved in ministry training.

A church will have to decide on a specified curriculum and uniform standards of performance for members who are to be credentialed. Many conferences have already established such a standard with the Lay Bible Minister Program. Those thus credentialed must have completed a certain amount of training, have been involved in Bible studies or similar ministry, and have successfully won some soul to Christ during the year. What we are suggesting here is that this process happen on the local level, as well.

It may be that some conferences will wish to establish uniform standards for the conference and even to issue credentials from the conference. That is all right, provided that credentialing gets recognition at the local level, because this is what will motivate others to get involved in training. However, the training events themselves are best done at the local level. Otherwise, there will be only limited impact on the local church. We need a higher critical mass of people who have been trained and are using that training in ministry if this whole process is to change the local church.

How to Begin

You may be asking about now, How do we get started? What I've read sounds good, but can we really pull it off in our little church? The answer is Yes, but it will take commitment and dedication. As you have read these pages, it should be obvious by now that we are talking about major changes in the way we approach church. No longer is church someplace to go on Sabbath morning; it becomes instead a vital component in each member's life. If your church is not committed to this revolution of making the laity the church, no amount of training will work. But if you are committed to this new style of church, you will find a way to make it work.

Begin by researching other churches that have a lay training program. Discover what they have done right, as well as what they did that didn't work. Ask them what they would do differently. Remember, what works in one situation doesn't work in all places. Don't copy someone else, but learn from them.

You may wish to start with just one or two courses and gradually add more as your program develops. Make sure you select the best teachers you can find, as well as courses of general interest at the beginning. Plan for success. Then publicize your courses to the church members and to the community, if appropriate. Your own Lay Ministry Committee may wish to think through additional steps in the process.

Lay training! What an exciting adventure awaits your local church! Remember that it begins with commitment and a willingness to move beyond the status quo. We are talking about returning the church to its biblical roots, where the laity is the church and the pastor is the trainer of the laity. This means new roles for both pastor and laity. We need to be charitable with each other in the transition to the new model. With plenty of love and grace, our churches can come alive, with laity on fire for Christ and desiring to share the everlasting gospel with the whole world. Then Jesus will come. May that day be soon!

11

Getting Started

Opening the ministry to the laity, having pastors who train instead of perform, discovering spiritual gifts, deploying people into ministry, training them—has all of this given you indigestion? Relax. You can't do it all at once. The Laodicean slumber of the North American church was not created in ten simple steps. Neither will the change back to the biblical model be accomplished easily. It may take years for some churches to undo what has happened over the last seventy-five years. But a beginning must take place under the guidance and direction of the Holy Spirit.

That beginning must commence with much prayer that the Holy Spirit will truly lead the church into Heaven-sent renewal. This renewal must enable the church to return to the New Testament and the early Adventist model of the church. There must also be heartfelt desire on the part of the church and its leadership to return to the biblical ideal of a church where the laity perform ministry, instead of only the pastors.

Lest what has been suggested in the previous pages be misunderstood, it should be strongly emphasized that in no church should the pastor simply stop doing ministry and expect the laity to take over. The shock would be so great that it would most likely destroy the church. Just as there was a gradual move away from the ideal, so the move back must be a gradual one. Yet there must be movement in the right direction.

Since the only pastoral care occurring in most churches is that given by the pastor, none would occur if the pastor stopped providing it. If that should happen, members of the church would not be cared for, and irreparable damage would be done to the body of Christ. Therefore it is imperative that the pastor continue to provide the present level of care until an adequate number of people are trained.

As lay pastors are trained and equipped to provide pastoral care, the pastor can reduce the time he devotes to that aspect of ministry and use the time saved to train members for other ministry. This will be a slow process at first, but as people become trained, the process will be accelerated. The pastor in the new model will never run out of things to do. He will be doing different things, but he will still be busy.

How does the pastor train people to care? In this transitional phase, the church should provide the training mentioned in the previous chapter. This formal training, vital as it is, will not suffice to equip people for ministry. In addition, there must be hands-on training occurring in the church. Every time the pastor makes a visit, be it pastoral or evangelistic, he should take a lay person with him. Let the lay person observe, then let the lay person do it while the pastor observes.

They should debrief themselves about the visit afterward so that insights are shared and the lay person grows in the ability to perform this ministerial function. After the lay person has gained a certain degree of proficiency, the pastor can dispatch the layperson on his own, remaining available for counsel and help. The layperson then takes another layperson with him, whom he trains in the same way that he (or she) was trained. The pastor likewise moves on to train another. Now two are being trained at once. As this process increases, the level of competency will grow, and a strong group of trained lay pastors will be developed. This supervised, practical experience is the only suitable method of training.

For too long the Adventist church has depended on weekend seminars to train its people. These are excellent and should continue. Yet on-the-job training can no longer be neglected. People must learn from pastors who actually mentor them. The reason this method has not been successful in the past is primarily because most pastors have never themselves been mentored. They have been told what to do, but never shown how to do it. Pastoral education of the future must focus on an integration of knowledge and the practical use of that knowledge. Only as pastors are trained in this manner will they learn how to train their members in practical ministry.

It would be ideal if the North American church would revert to its roots; then there would not be settled pastors over the churches. It would be more like the third world model. While this may be ideal, we must recognize, realistically, that this probably will not happen. We have gone too far down the road. We are too dependent on the pastors. Yet God has not forsaken us; He can start us down the road to new beginnings.

The Church of the Future

The church of the twenty-first century may well be larger than has been common with Adventists. Yet in certain ways it will actually be smaller, because people will be ministered to as if they were in a small church. The activities of the pastor in this large church will differ from those of pastors today. That pastor will be directing the laity in their multitudinous ministries. The pastor's time will be spent, not so much in performing ministerial functions, as in training and supervising the laity. Thus, even if a pastor is settled over a church, his job description will be vastly different from current pastoral practice, and he will be more in harmony with the biblical ideal.

The Adventist church of the twenty-first century will be larger, yet smaller. The reason for this is that the church will function on a small-group basis rather than on a congregational model. Most present church structure is built around one pastor ministering to a congregation of anywhere from twenty-five to a thousand people. In the church of the future, a pastor will supervise small-group leaders, who will in turn lead groups of ten to twelve people. These lay pastors will be the primary caregivers in the church. The clergy will pastor the lay pastors, and they in turn will pastor the people. The membership will be better cared for by the lay pastors than by the ordained pastor, simply because they will have only ten to twelve people in their care system. The most any one ordained clergy person can pastor adequately is about fifty people. The reason the pastoral care system fails so often is that most pastors have congregations of more than fifty people.

In training people for the church of the future, the primary training event will be to equip the leaders of the small groups. These lay pastors will in turn train the members of their small groups to nurture one another and to evangelize their friends and neighbors. In the twenty-first century church setting, it will be as necessary to belong to a small group as it now is to be present on Sabbath morning. In fact, people would not be regarded as members in good and regular standing unless they were involved in small groups.

The proliferation of small groups in the twenty-first century church will necessitate the training of many lay pastors to lead and care for these groups. The large variety of ministries the small groups generate will create the need for the training programs of the future. As we discussed training in the last chapter, some might have wondered what everyone will be doing. What are the new ministries in which people will be involved? These will mostly be centered in the small groups of the church.

Why Small Groups?

The small-group movement sweeping America today is destined to totally revolutionize the church of the future. It is not a passing fad, but a return to our biblical and Adventist roots.

The early church did not assemble in grand cathedrals; the early believers, instead, met mostly in homes. Houses of worship were not erected to any large extent until centuries after the early apostles had died. Since the meeting places of the early church were the homes of the believers, it then was necessary that these churches had to be small groups. (See Romans 16:5; 1 Corinthians 16:19; Colossians 4:15; Philemon 2.)

Clearly, the early church was organized on a small-group principle, with a lay elder over the group. Pastors, as we know them today, did not exist. The clergy were the apostles and missionaries, who went everywhere starting up new churches, appointing lay elders over the churches to care for the believers, and then moving on to start other churches. As these early churches grew, and as the church degenerated, pastors were eventually hired to care for the churches because of the increased number of members. Ideally, the church should have formed new groups and continued to grow instead of hiring pastors. Once pastors took over, the level of care available to the flock dropped dramatically.

The early Adventist church followed the New Testament pattern very closely. While most early Adventist churches were small groups headed by lay elders, they soon grew into congregations. Yet as we have seen, for nearly fifty years after its organization and even after the churches grew, Adventism did not have settled pastors. Pastors evangelized, and the churches were cared for by lay elders.

How good was the care in these early Adventist churches? While we don't have any real records of the care given, one can only assume that the care was superior to that given today, because apostasies were dramatically fewer. How did they do it?

The early Adventists attended three basic services each week. Every Sabbath found them in the church with a body of believers praising God. This would be the same service that we today recognize as the 11 o'clock worship service on Sabbath morning. This provided them with the feeling that they belonged to a body of believers. This conviction was strengthened by the camp meeting, where early Adventists would join hundreds and thousands of others in an annual time of worship. They needed this special time, especially if they belonged to a small church. It helped them realize that they belonged to something much larger than the small group at their home church. And even if the home church was large, this annual convocation helped members feel that they were part of a much larger group.

In addition to the worship hour and the camp meeting, the early Adventists attended Sabbath School each week. This was recognized as a period for the study of the Word. The Sabbath School ministered to the intellectual needs of the believer. Its primary emphasis was on the intellectual development of the Christian. Sabbath School discussions provided the cognitive orientation to the church that Adventists needed.

Yet early Adventists were not satisfied with collective worship and the intellectual stimulation afforded by the Sabbath School alone. They saw that Adventism must be concerned not only with the mental development of the believer but also with the emotional, or social nature. In fact, they regarded the harmonious development of one's physical, mental, social, and spiritual faculties to be the essence of true education.

How did they care for social development? Through small groups. Essential to an understanding of the growth of early Adventism is the understanding of the role small groups played. While Sabbath School, as a small group, cared for their intellectual development, there was another small-group meeting which met their relational needs as well. Early Adventists called these "social meetings."

Not all of their time in these social meetings was spent studying the Bible for cognitive information—Sabbath School accomplished that. In fact, many times there may have been little Bible study. It seems that the purpose of these small groups was to help members grow spiritually. They dealt, therefore, with the relational needs of the members and held members spiritually accountable. They prayed, they sang, and they bore their testimony to each other. Note how Ellen White describes the activities of these early Adventist small-group social meetings:

> All should have something to say for the Lord, for by so doing they will be blest.—*Early Writings*, p. 114.

> We should not come together to remain silent; those only are remembered of the Lord who assemble to speak of His honor and glory and tell of His power; upon such the blessing of God will rest, and they will be refreshed.—*Early Writings,* p. 115.

> Some hold back in meeting because they have nothing new to say and must repeat the same story if they speak. I saw that pride was at the bottom of this, that God and angels witnessed the testimonies of the saints and were well pleased and glorified by their being repeated weekly.—*Early Writings*, p. 115.

> At every social meeting many testimonies were borne as to the peace, comfort, and joy the people had found in receiving light.—*Selected Messages*, book one, p. 356.

A quick examination of these statements by Ellen White reveals that she considered the social meeting to be a special time for the people of God to spend together. Note that the time was not to be spent discussing doctrine or even in Bible study. The primary function of the social meeting was the relational edification of the believers. In a chapter entitled "Social Meetings," Ellen White describes the purpose of these meetings:

> What is the object of assembling together? Is it to inform God, to instruct Him by telling Him all we know in prayer? We meet together to edify one another by an interchange of thoughts and feelings, to gather strength, and light, and courage by becoming acquainted with one another's hopes and aspirations; and by our earnest, heartfelt prayers, offered up in faith, we receive refreshment and vigor from the Source of our strength. These meetings should be most precious seasons and should be made interesting to all who have any relish for religious things. —*Testimonies for the Church*, vol. 2, p. 578.

Somehow as Adventism grew, we lost the social meeting. We retained the corporate worship and Sabbath School function, but we lost the personal edification to be found in small-group social meetings. Once again today, there is a strong movement in Adventism to recover the small-group emphasis of the early Adventists.

However, some have misunderstood the purpose of the small groups and have turned them into a cognitive Bible study similar to a Sabbath School class. When this happens, the small group is not fulfilling the relational function that the social meeting did in early Adventism.

Part of the genius of the Adventist movement has been the blend of the physical, mental, social or relational, and spiritual. That's why the small-group function is such a necessary ingredient of the modern church that seeks to reach the whole person.

Why have we diverted our discussion into small groups in this chapter? Precisely because the small-group experience will necessitate the training of many new small-group leaders in the church. These groups will be relational rather than cognitive. This will demand the training of a new kind of leader. Most of our present lay leadership know how to lead cognitive groups, but few have been trained in the skills needed for relational groups.

Since these relational groups are the place where people share their life in Christ with each other, the place where members and newcomers both receive affirmation and discipleship, the leaders of these small groups are actually lay pastors who assist the pastor in the care of the flock. If the church is to return to God's plan for it, in which the laity instead of the pastor cares for the flock, then the small-group approach must be utilized, even as it was in the early days of Adventism. At that time, the laity additionally pastored the churches, leaving the preachers free to evangelize and raise up new congregations.

As we move back to the biblical model, the pastor will need to train his small-group leaders in conducting relational, caring, small groups. As leaders are thus equipped, the pastor can release them into the caring ministry of the church. The pastor will need to meet with them at least once a week; however, now the members will be adequately cared for, and the pastor will be free to train others and evangelize.

Ideally, the small, caring group is also the perfect place to bring new people. In my experience, I have discovered that we rarely lose a person who joins a small group. Why? Because the relational bridges have been built. Most of our assimilation of new members has been doctrinal, though few people leave because of doctrine. The reason for the loss of members is relational. Small, relational groups could be a big help to us in stemming the tide of apostasy. Even before people join the church, they should be involved in a small group, so that relational ties are built from the very beginning.

Putting It All Together

In summary, a church that wishes to rekindle the flame of early Adventism should seek to incorporate as many of the following steps as possible:

■ A time to pray for the Holy Spirit and a revival of primitive godliness in the church.

■ A rediscovery of the role of the laity as the performer of ministry in the church.

■ A recommissioning of the pastor as the trainer/equipper of people in the church. This becomes the chief responsibility of the pastor.

■ A discovery of the spiritual gifts of the members.

■ A placing of people into ministry in harmony with their spiritual gifts.

■ An ongoing training program for the church, providing the skills needed for various ministries.

■ An on-the-job training program to supplement the formal training.

■ A system of small groups to provide for the relational needs of the members.

Adventism that is approaching the twenty-first century has wandered from its beginnings. We are troubled by the stagnancy of the church today. Perhaps we need to return to our roots. This return will involve three main areas:

■ Restoring ministry to laity

■ Reeducating pastors to be trainers instead of performers

■ Establishing small relational groups for member care

As these three things happen, the church will once again become a place where people can freely share their life in Christ. Out of this, Adventism can once more move the world in preparation for the return of our Lord.

Let's begin now!